The Underground Guide
to
Los Angeles

3rd edition

Pleasant Gehman & Iris Berry
Editors

Manic D Press
San Francisco

Dedicated to the memory of
Cow "Dingbat" Brown
Spring 1999 - April 2, 2006
R.I.P.

Special thanks and extreme gratitude to Ed for being an amazing sister, Natasha and Kelly, Augie, Amy Kelly and Sonia, Lindaloo, James "Dirt Basket" Packard, Tony "Yarnmouth" Malone always, Vivien Kooper, Chris Martin, Amanda Toland, The Ringling Sisters, Danny Dempsey, Iris's whole entire family, Lisa Derrek, The Brooklyn, everyone at Moun of Tunis, everyone at the Edendale Grill, Joe Donnelly, and to Victor's Deli, where most of this book was written.

Also to Skylight Books which has always been so supportive, to all the writers who contributed their time and considerable talents to this project, and most especially to Jen Joseph and Manic D Press.

EVER-LOVIN' DISCLAIMER: Just as almost everything in life is negotiable, so too everything is conditional and SUBJECT TO CHANGE without a moment's notice. A listing in this book does not imply endorsement. All opinions are those of the individual authors, and not necessarily those of the publisher or editors. All information is allegedly accurate as this goes to print but, hey, deal with it, okay? If you find something here that just ain't so, please be kind enough to let us know.

All chapters not credited to someone else were written by Pleasant Gehman!

© 2006 Manic D Press, Inc. All rights reserved. No part of this book may be used or reproduced in any manner whatsoever without written permission of the publisher except in the case of brief quotations embodied in critical articles or reviews. Contact Manic D Press, PO Box 410804, San Francisco CA 94141. www.manicdpress.com.
ISBN-10: 1-933149-14-0 / ISBN-13: 978-1-933149-14-1
Cover: Scott Idleman / BLINK   Illustrations: P. Gehman

– Contents –

FORWARD!

City of the Angels, Tinseltown, Hell-A, El Lay... whatever you want to call it, Los Angeles is a fabulous, glamorous, unique place — after all, there's gotta be a reason so many people are still here after all the earthquakes, fires, mudslides, floods, and riots, right? We are both Native Angelenos: Iris was born here, Pleasant is a common-law native, having lived here for more than thirty years. We lived together in Hollywood in the 1980s, when it was safe to sleep with your ground-floor windows open! Those days are long gone, and even though LA is getting unbelievably crowded and we have both fantasized about leaving for years, we wouldn't even consider acting upon it. Hollywood is in our DNA. Los Angeles — no matter what anyone says — is not a cultural wasteland. It's an amazing, invigorating place.

Like the previous editions, this is by no means a complete guide — hey, could there ever REALLY be one? But this outrageously opinionated opus is compiled writings — a couple of updates, but mostly brand spankin' new chapters — from resident Angelenos. The motley crew who contributed are writers, artists, musicians, activists, ultra-hip scenesters, and professional bonvivants who know the best places to eat, drink, buy cheap vintage clothes, get body parts inked, pierced or massaged, see (or show) great art, hear new bands, see great theater and meet foxy, like-minded folk... all on a shoestring budget! There's even a chapter telling you who to call if you get towed, arrested, or are in need of rehab. Years of collective research went into the making of this guide. Some of the entries will be familiar, and some are serendipitous secrets divulged for the first time.

Because of the city's sprawling nature, you may want to rent a car. LA's transportation system (MTA buses, subways, light rail) is extensive, but awfully time-consuming. You may be stranded at a stop for ages between transfers, or stuck in our famous gridlock traffic. Cabs are plentiful but expensive. As with any major city, crime is a problem. Please don't be fooled by lovely pastel houses with manicured lawns and tropical flowers — any neighborhood can be a "bad" neighborhood, so keep your guard. Pick up a freeway map, or, better yet, purchase an invaluable **Thomas Guide** (a complete and coded LA street map) at a bookstore. You should also grab a copy of *The LA Weekly* or *City Beat* (free alternative newspapers) for current entertainment listings. Another free fishwrap, *The Recycler*, has classified ads for apartment rentals, used cars, musical equipment, pets, jobs, and what-have-you. They're all published every Thursday. Please note that LA's area codes are 213 and 323 (greater Los Angeles), 310 (Westside), 818 (San Fernando Valley), and 626 (San Gabriel Valley). So... explore and enjoy!

Big Hollywood air-kisses,
Pleasant Gehman & Iris Berry

P.S. Several places get mentioned in more than one chapter — sometimes with differences of opinion! If a place crops up often, it's probably worth investigating — decide for yourself if it stinks or is great.

WHEREVER I HANG MY HAT
Places to Stay

Los Angeles, unfortunately, is not full of inexpensive, clean, safe places to stay. It's usually better to call up pals or a friend of a friend and see if you can crash for a while. There are, however, a few options that won't break your bank or scare you to death. If you have Internet access, discounted room rates are often available online. A word to the wise, though there are plenty of decent, inexpensive places to stay near LAX, you will definitely be traveling *at least* half an hour to get anywhere.

USA HOSTELS HOLLYWOOD (1624 Schraeder Blvd., Hollywood, 800-524-6783 or 323-462-3777, usahostels.com) Finally, a hostel that's actually walking distance from things you'd want to see or do. This vintage Spanish-style lodging in the heart of Hollywood features free rides to and from the airport, bus and train stations, free parking, a beach shuttle, laundry, storage, DSL internet access, and a huge, fully equipped kitchen. They have free comedy shows once a week, pancake breakfasts, and linen service, too. They also have tours going to Mexico, Vegas, the Grand Canyon, and SoCal theme parks. Private rooms are $58-$64. FYI: This place books up fast, especially in the summer months, so plan accordingly.

BEST WESTERN HOLLYWOOD HILLS HOTEL (6141 Franklin Ave., Hollywood, 323-464-5181) Located in central Hollywood about a block and a half off the Boulevard of Broken Dreams, and a hop, skip and a jump away from the fun 'n' cool Franklin Strip, this hotel has large clean (though unremarkable) rooms with two double beds, air conditioning, TV, and phones starting at $149. There's also underground parking, a large pool, and a tragically hip coffee shop downstairs that serves great food at reasonable prices. Eat there and you'll also have the dubious pleasure of seeing, like, Deborah Messing (sans make-up) picking at a tofu scramble or Quentin Tarantino jabbering on his cell-phone while scarfing a burrito.

HOTEL ROOSEVELT (7000 Hollywood Blvd., Hollywood, 323-466-7000) is Hollywood's only historic hotel still in operation today and has been in business 79 years. Rooms starting at $179 (for a double or single room) and is full of old Hollywood glamour — and reputedly haunted — especially the ninth floor. Rumor has it that Johnette Napolitano of Concrete Blonde was thrown out one night for playing with an Ouija board near the elevator. Make sure you check out their poolside club **The Tropicana** with private cabanas and VIP bottle service. Celebrity sightings: Paris and Nicole... *not kidding*.

CHATEAU MARMONT (8221 W. Sunset Blvd., W. Hollywood, 323-656-1010, chateaumarmont.com) used to be THE place to stay for down-at-the-heels artists and rockers, but underwent a chi-chi facelift and is extremely expensive — $335 a night to start with! If you wanna go all movie star or you're on some record company's expense account, you can book the private bungalows for $1,700-$2,700 a night. Still, if you can swing it, you might see Drew Barrymore, Courtney Love or Leonardo Di Caprio at the gorgeous pool. It's probably better to just visit **Bar Marmont** and have a martini.

FARMER'S DAUGHTER MOTEL (115 S. Fairfax, LA, 323-937-3930, www.farmersdaughtermotel.com) in West Hollywood, located directly across the street from Farmer's Market, and the new Grove Mall, this place is clean and semi-reasonable, at $149 (for two people) per night. This would also be a good place to put up the folks.

PLANET VENICE BEACH HOSTEL (1515 Pacific Ave., Venice, 310-452-3052, pv@catrica.com) is out at the beach, full of itinerant Euro trash, but extremely reasonable at $29.75 per person for dorm rooms, $76.50 for a private room.

THE SHANGRI-LA HOTEL (1301 Ocean Ave., Santa Monica, 310-394-271, shangrila_hotel.com) is also by the beach, and is a classic Art Deco building. Most of the rooms are airy suites (some with ocean views, but you'll pay for that) and breakfast is included. It's a Rudolph Valentino kind of experience, with rooms ranging from $170-$235 per night.

Another option for long or shortish-term housing would be to drop by the **SCREEN ACTORS GUILD** (5757 Wilshire

Blvd., 213-954-1600, www.sag.org). There's a bulletin board with tons of rooms for rent, and sublets for apartments, houses, and condos, because so many actors are coming and going all the time.

For housing options/roommate situations, also check out **www.craigslist.org.**

A MINIATURE ETERNITY
Where to Eat
Suzy Beal

"A three-hour dinner to me is a miniature eternity,
no matter how good the food is. One of the reasons
is that while I'm waiting for the food to come, I have
to sit there and talk to people." — Frank Zappa

There are lots of excellent restaurants in LA — the famous,
the pricey, the pompous — all easy to find via word of mouth
advertising, and the latest TV tabloid scandal. Who needs 'em?
LA is also the home of fast food, drive-ins, carhops, and
experimental cuisine. Its spiritual pulse has always been along
the lines of the slightly outré. The places noted here are mostly
about breakfast, burgers, diners, dives, and culturally diverse
foods (Mexican, Italian, Asian...). Most are centrally located,

cheap-to-reasonable, and convenient to cultural centers and things to do. So have fun, and as they used to say at Millie's: Eat, pay, and get out.

LOCAL FAVORITES

CHILI JOHN'S (2018 W. Burbank Blvd., Burbank, 818-846-3611) a strangely bleak white '20s box of a place with a U-shaped counter, serving chili and pie. Period. Well, okay... chili alone, with beans or spaghetti, hot or not. That's it. Recipe for delirium: a 103-degree day plus a hangover plus lunch here...

ALEGRIA (3510 Sunset Blvd., 323-913-1422) One of those strip mall sleepers that serves really delicious gourmet Mexican food at strip mall prices. Soft taco combinations, swordfish, tender meats in subtle sauces, appealing vegetarian plates. Top-notch regional cooking, dinners $3.99 & up.

CIRO'S (705 N. Evergreen, East LA, 323-269-5104) A truly great Eastside diner with a swell jukebox, killer salsa, friendly vibes, and world-famous taquitos (a half-order is about $3 and comes with beans, rice and salad). Order a little more and get the terrific guacamole gratis.

MI & MI (various locations) Casual outdoor seating and lots of good fresh Middle Eastern dishes. The combo salad plates include falafel, hummus, tabbouleh, baba ghanouj, mushroom salad, pickles, olives and bread; about 30-50% cheaper than similar places.

MAKO (1820 N. Vermont Ave., Los Feliz) No sign, no phone, no clue you're here, but the line at the little place just under the Los Feliz Theatre marquee speaks loudly: casual Japanese cafe food (teriyaki, sushi, soup) and unheard-of prices, $2-5. Hits the spot.

EMPRESS PAVILION (Bamboo Plaza, 988 N. Hill St., 323-617-9898) Really fun dim sum brunch in a large, fairly elegant room in Chinatown: passing carts dole out dumplings, chicken feet, etc. (You may search in vain for rice or vegetables—it's all meat, sauce, sugar'n'starch). Add a cocktail and enter a guaranteed 2-day stupor.

SENOR FISH (422 E. 1st St., at Alameda, 323-625-0566. Other locations in Eagle Rock, South Pasadena, Boyle Heights.) The latest branch of everyone's favorite fish taco place is in, of all places, the old Atomic Cafe—the ghosts of punk rock and baloney chop suey barely disturb the aura of happiness around the plates of fish, shrimp and scallop tacos with cabbage, salsa and crema $1.35 & up.

LA LUZ DEL DIA (1 West Olvera St., 323-628-7495) At the south end of Olvera Street, La Luz serves up various Mexican combination plates for $5 or less. Great carnitas and handmade tortillas, home-cooked beans; charming tiled dining room and patio.

BURRITO KING (2109 W. Sunset Blvd, 323-413-9444) other locations throughout LA) In a world of burrito places, here is the archetype. Corner stand serving great big delicious burritos— some like the veg version with lots of beans, cheese, guac, etc; others swear by *machaca* or beef or pork versions. Cheap.

INSTITUTIONS
...And who'd want to dine in an institution? If you're from LA, you already eat in these places because they're great, or you know people there, or the drinks are cheap, or... you have to. If you're a visitor, well, knowing these places is practically a requirement.

EL COYOTE (7312 Beverly Blvd., 323-939-7766) Gaudy, tacky, and cheap Cal-Mex fare. Bright decor and, uh, brown food. People come here because it's cheap and the drinks knock you on your ass. (Order margaritas from scratch.) The green corn tamales are edible. (Editors' note: after a couple of El Coyote margaritas EVERYTHING including the velvet paintings, fake flowers and glass grapes, strings of Christmas lights are edible and maybe even preferable!)

PHILIPPE (1001 N. Alameda St., 323-628-3781) Downtown's beloved French dip place with sawdust on the floor and famous ten-cent coffee. Fresh roast beef, pork or lamb sandwiches (in the $3 range) plus lots of sides, pie, pickled eggs, and wooden phone booths.

PINK'S (709 N. La Brea Ave., 323-931-4223) Famous Chili Dogs. Another landmark everyone has seen on TV at some point; of course the dogs are good and range from mild to caustic, but there is a system: 1 dog=yum, 2 dogs=okay; 3 dogs (shoved down)=instantaneous projectile vomiting. (I don't know why, but it works like a charm.) Amaze your friends!

TOMMY'S BURGERS (2575 Beverly Blvd., 323-389-9060) Anyone who claims to know LA is required to eat here, it's the granddaddy of all burger shacks. People line up far into the night to inhale these delicious grease bombs. A weirdly incandescent SRO parking lot scene is surrounded by acres of crime...

CLIFTON'S CAFETERIA (648 S. Broadway, Downtown LA, 323-627-1673) LA's most famous and peculiar Depression-era cafeteria with a North Woods theme: waterfalls, fake moon over redwoods, plus a teensy castle with a religious diorama inside. Serves your basic meat, casseroles, and breakfasts, $2-4. They have a nice historical website at www.cliftonscafeteria.com

DAMON'S (317 N. Brand Blvd., Glendale, 818-507-1510) Meat, potatoes and Mai Tais. This Polynesian steakhouse has been serving the above since 1937, with a suitably modest set of sides: decent shrimp cocktails and a famously odd dressing on the salad. Old-fashioned prices, too.

VERSAILLES (10319 Venice Blvd., 310-558-3168) More lines, despite the presence of a second Versailles on La Cienega. But folks sure go for that garlicky roast chicken and pork, black beans, rice, and plantains. Entrees start around $4. Seafood and paella, too.

CHEZ JAY (1657 Ocean Av., Santa Monica, 310-395-1741) Fancy beach dive: big steaks, lobsters, good drinks, Sinatra on the jukebox.

FORMOSA CAFE (7156 Santa Monica Blvd., 323-850-9050) This ancient railroad car bar'n'restaurant creaks on, literally haunted by the shades of Gable, Monroe, Bogart... Food is just as creepy. But what atmosphere! Especially after a couple of their killer martinis or mai tais! (Editors' note: no decorations worth eating here, but hundreds of signed historic movie star 8x10s.)

BIG FOOD AND OTHER BARGAINS
LA ADELITA (5812 Santa Monica Blvd., Hollywood, 323-465-6526) A Mexican pastry shop/deli in the strip mall that flanks the venerable **Hollywood Forever Memorial Park**,

La Adelita makes hearty stews and tortas: huge sandwiches chock full o' roasted pork, turkey or beef, garnished with beans, lettuce, onion and salsa. A total bargain at about $3. (Eat 'em next door among the monuments of Hollywood's storied dead.)

DINAH'S (6521 Sepulveda Blvd., Culver City, 310-645-0456. Plus other locations.) A landmark family coffee shop. Famous for fried chicken, cheap specials, and laughably huge German pancakes (about a foot wide and crammed with apple stuff). Deviate from the specials at your fiscal peril. Fun place to gorge.

THE ORIGINAL PANTRY (877 S. Figueroa Ave., Downtown LA, 323-972-9279) Open 24 hours and handy for late night meals. Famous for an enormous steak or chop dinners, unfinishably large breakfasts and welcome crocks of fresh crudités at the table as well as ancient ex-con waiters. Reasonable, considering the pounds of food you get (though profits enrich owner/ex-Mayor Richard Riordan).

AUTHENTIC CAFE (7605 Beverly Blvd., 323-939-4626) Insanely busy Southwestern/Pacific/"creative" low-cost cuisine in funky setting. People keep coming like zombies; it has everything people can tolerate in terms of flavor and price.

EL TEPEYEC (812 N. Evergreen Ave., East LA, 323-267-8668) Yet another LA institution, but also a bargain palace! Most customers are second-generation natives, locals, and City Hall types. Cheery and busy with unpretentious Mexican food, including the famous Hollenbeck Burrito, literally large enough to feed four. If you can eat two, they'll give you another free. (If you eat three I think they pay for the ambulance.) (Editors' note: Yet another place to amaze your friends!)

ALGEMAC'S (3673 San Fernando Road, Glendale, 818-240-8626) 1930s coffeeshop serving comfort food and good breakfasts in the $2.50-$5 range. Located across from **Forest Lawn Cemetery**, which makes it convenient for celebrity crypt-hunting trips.

PORTO'S BAKERY (315 N. Brand Blvd., Glendale, 818-956-5996) A large, airy bakery/sandwich shop with excellent inexpensive Cuban and American pastries, Cuban sandwiches, salady things, and small hot items — croquettes, meat-and-mashed-potato balls, meat pies — for pocket change. Ever heard of hot food for 35-70 cents? Now you have.

LA CABANITA (3447 N. Verdugo Rd., Glendale, 818-957-2711) Recently voted best taco in LA (if such a thing is even possible in the world capitol of Mexican food), this cozy place in the Glendale foothills is worth the drive. Several kinds of tacos, all different and all amazing — when we tried them we literally laughed out loud with pleasure, and we weren't drunk!

BREAKFAST AND LIGHT MEALS

PANTRY BAKERY AND SANDWICH SHOP (875 S. Figueroa St., Downtown LA, 213-972-9279) Yep, it's that place directly north and attached to the regular Pantry. Why there are two, who knows? It's more breakfasty than the steaky Original Pantry next door, plus burgers, melts, flapjacks, and big portions. Reasonable.

RAE'S (2901 Pico Blvd., Santa Monica, 310-828-7937) The extremely stylish turquoise 1950s diner Americans have seen in countless videos and films. But it's real roadside food: cottage fries, biscuits, sandwiches, and cheerfully low-key.

As great as it looks, it's no Le Dome, but still one of the few genuine diners in LA.

DU-PAR'S (12036 Ventura Blvd. at Fairfax, LA, 323-933-8446) Kind of run-of-the-mill '50s coffeeshop but rabid fans like their understandably famous breakfasts and pies: blueberry cream cheese, apple, pecan, strawberry. Celebrity sightings: Sandra Bernhardt and Heidi Fleiss, not dining together.

ROSCOE'S CHICKEN AND WAFFLES (1514 N. Gower St., Hollywood, 323-466-7453, other locations) Talk about your heart attack on a plate! But what a delicious way to go: enormous pieces of fried chicken, mashed potatoes, grits, greens... and waffles drenched in butter and syrup. Celebrity sightings: Peppa (of Salt n' Peppa), members of the Lakers, Gary Coleman. Not dining together.

MILLIE'S (3828 W. Sunset Blvd., Silverlake, 323-664-0404) Everyone eats here sooner or later. Vintage diner serving big breakfasts with garlicky rosemary cottage fries, strong coffee, biscuits and gravy plus a swell old jukebox. Super popular with Silverlake and Hollywood types. Thankfully, the newest owners don't think it's "cute" to berate and throw things at customers, as was the fashion here, so all can feel welcome.

UNCLE BILL'S PANCAKE HOUSE (1305 Highland Ave., Manhattan Beach, 310-545-8777) The long wait tells you the huge breakfasts, waffles with cheese and bacon, etc., are just what the doctor ordered. Especially when you add juicy burgers and big ol' dinners...

MUSSO AND FRANK'S GRILL (6667 Hollywood Blvd., Hollywood, 323-467-5123) "The Oldest Restaurant in

Hollywood" (think Hammett, Fitzgerald, et al) can also have an attitude that gets old at times. Expensive, too, but two people can order a bacon and egg breakfast, excellent coffee, and the famous Flannel Cakes, and share. The latter tastes like big soft fortune cookies and is one of the menu's real bargains.

101 COFFEE SHOP (6145 Franklin Ave., Hollywood, 323-467-7678) Situated at a motor hotel, featured in the movie *Swingers*, it's got a noisy, retro/wacky interior and a youngish crowd. Big portions.

JOHN O'GROAT'S (10516 W. Pico Blvd., 310-204-0692) The Lincoln Monument of breakfast places. Fresh biscuits, pork chops. People swear (albeit politely) by this place; now serving home-style weekend dinners.

THE TOASTED BUN (808 E. California St., Glendale, 818-244-6416) Indifferent coffeeshop, but it's edible in a dustbowl way, and it's fun to have someone meet you at The Toasted Bun.

BAKERIES
CELAYA BAKERY (1630 W. Sunset Blvd., LA, 213-250-2472) Mexican *panaderia* specializing in fabulous fresh bread rolls (this is where restaurants buy 'em). 20 cents each!
THE BACK DOOR BAKERY (1710 N. Silver Lake Blvd., 323-662-7927) Where everyone in Silver Lake goes for Apple Uglies, Lemon Sex, real Hostess Cupcakes and dee-licious breakfasts.

OLD TOWN BAKERY (166 W. Colorado Blvd, Pasadena, 818-793-2993) Chocolate Chocolate Chocolate Cake. (It's 3-layer classic devil's food with bittersweet icing and ganache.)

THE COBBLER FACTORY (33 N. Catalina Ave., Pasadena, 626-449-2152) Old-timey handmade hot cobblers of pretty much any type fruit you can think of. Reasonable, too.

BROOKLYN BAGEL BAKERY (2217 W. Beverly Blvd. LA, 213-413- 4114) This is where lots of restaurants order their supposedly homemade bagels — go there yourself and get the freshest, warmest bagels in town.

FOOD TO GO!
MONTE CARLO'S PINNOCHIO RESTAURANT (3103 West Magnolia Blvd., Burbank, 818-845-3516) Regular homey sitdown place, but with large buffet counter chock fulla old-fashioned Italian food you can take out. More than you can finish, and reasonable.

BBQ KING (867 W. Sunset Blvd., LA, 213-972-1928) Beef ribs, hot links, spicy beans, tri-tip, chili cheese fries. Run by Texas folks. It's kind of a shack, but you can eat in if you really want to...

HAPPY HOUR!
McCORMICK AND SCHMICK'S (First Interstate Towers, 633 W. 5th St., 213-629-1929) Clubby upscale place at top of picturesque steps above the Central Library, but at Happy Hour they serve a bunch of $1.95 specials truly worth the trip: calamari, dim sum, oysters, mini cheeseburgers, etc. Plus strong drinks.

BARRAGAN'S (1538 Sunset Blvd., Echo Park, 213-250-4256) Yes, good ol' Barragan's! Still the most comfortable and consistent family restaurant in the Echo Park/Silver Lake area. Don't forget they got yer $2-3 beers and margaritas, plus complimentary nachos.

HIP HANGOUTS & AFTER HOURS

DAMIANO'S MR. PIZZA (412 N. Fairfax Ave., LA, 323-658-8761) Dark, teensy, New Yorkish, deep booths to hide in, open late: Damiano's is a port in a storm for locals. Lots of imported beers, pasta dinners and reasonable prices.

CANTER'S (419 N. Fairfax Ave., LA, 323-651-2030) An LA institution, serving semi-pricey (but authentic) deli fare. What draws the kids is the adjacent lounge with live music and the long hours where dates can wind down with coffee and terrific pastries.

SWINGER'S (8020 Beverly Blvd., LA, 213-653-5858) Swinger's has gone from excruciatingly hip to institution status, sort of. Corn pancakes in jalapeno syrup, tofu scramble American food – these'll help distract you from your too hip dining mates.

TORUNG (5657 Hollywood Blvd., Hollywood, 213-464-9074) Everyone knows this isn't the greatest Thai place in town, but we sometimes need a bowl of Tom Ka Kai at 3 a.m., and Torung has been meeting this need for years. Comfy booths, fish tanks, television, and an endless menu with most items $4-6. Dicey neighborhood, and street towing after 1 a.m.

DUKE'S COFFEE SHOP (8909 Sunset Blvd., Hollywood, 310-652-3100) No longer located in the landmark Tropicana Motel (which was razed years ago), Duke's nonetheless oozes history from its previous incarnations as Sneeky Pete's and the London Fog (The Doors played here, of course). Folks share communal tables or a counter and eat really satisfying breakfasts, especially yummy pancakes with added fruit and goop. Average prices.

JOSEPH'S CAFE (1775 N. Ivar St., Hollywood, 323-462-8697) Breakfast is kind of underwhelming but the Greek items are quite good: *tarama*, *feta* and spinach snacks, Greek salads. It's also cool, relaxing, neat as a pin and low-key. At night it transforms into, of all things, a popular nightclub with DJs and dancing. The best of both worlds. (Editors' note: Celebrity sighting: Jessica Simpson and Britney Spears falling in the gutter. Not drinking together.)

PATRICK'S ROADHOUSE (106 Entrada Dr., Santa Monica, 310-459-4544) Beach dive for dining and stargazing. Burgers and breakfast. If movie stars make you sick, don't go there. Food's good, though.

THE SHACK (185 Culver Blvd., Playa del Rey, 310-823-6222) Well-named beach place serving burgers, beer, chili, and the Shack Burger: 1/4 lb. patty with Louisiana sausage. Full bar.

JAY'S JAYBURGER (4481 Santa Monica Blvd., LA, 323-666-5204) Big. Gooey. Messy. Yummy. Chili. Probably in the top 3 rated burger stands in LA.

CASA BIANCA (1650 Colorado Blvd., Eagle Rock, 323-256-9617) Generations of locals love the old-timey taste and ambiance, but it's about more than nostalgia here — the pizzas are really excellent.

MAURICE'S SNACK'N'CHAT (5549 W. Pico Blvd., LA, 323-931-3877) Fried chicken, short ribs, smothered pork chops, pan-fried fish; it all tastes home-cooked, which must be why people are drawn here like hungry kids. It can't be the prices, best described as moderate.

AUNT KIZZY'S BACK PORCH (4325 Glencoe Ave., Marina Del Rey, 310-578-1005) More well-regarded soul food on the West Side.

SUEHIRO CAFE (337 E. 1st St., Downtown LA, 213-626-9132) Spotless yet casual Japanese cafe near the Temporary Contemporary Museum of Art. Noodle bowls to teriyaki to huge trays of sushi, cutlets, dumplings, salads, tempura, and fried fish. Quite reasonable.

LA SERENATA DE GARIBALDI (1842 E. 1st St., Boyle Heights, 323-265-2887, also two locations in West LA) A universe of fresh fish dishes with incredible sauces of amazing variety and hue. Even broke locals go here for a special occasion. It's not the cheapest place in the world, but it is astoundingly delicious.

LA PARILLA (2126 E. Cesar Chavez Blvd., Boyle Heights, 213-262-3434) Bring a group and dive into a feast of table-grilled meats, guacamole, tortillas and sides. Affordable.

EMERGENCY AND HEALTH LA

Police, Fire, Ambulance (Emergency): 911
Poison Control Center: 800-876-4766, 24 hours
AIDS Information Hotline: 800-922-AIDS
National Runaway Switchboard: 800-621-4000
Child Abuse Hotline: 800-540-4000
LA County Domestic Violence Hotline: 800-978-3600
LA Suicide Prevention Hot Line: 310-391-1253
Rape and Battery Hotline: 213-626-3393
Alcoholics Anonymous: 323-936-4343
Narcotics Anonymous: 323-933-5395
Red Cross Disaster Services: 213-739-5200, 24 hours

LA Free Clinic (Three locations: 8405 Beverly Blvd., W. Hollywood, 6043 Hollywood Blvd., Hollywood, 5205 Melrose, LA, 323-653-1990 or 323-462-4158.) Sexually transmitted diseases, flu shots, dental care, general healthcare. Call for appointment, no walk-ins.

Hollywood-Sunset Free Clinic (3324 Sunset Blvd., 323-660-5715) appointment scheduling: Mondays, Wednesdays & Fridays, 10 a.m. - noon) General medical care, family planning and birth control, STD and HIV testing, gynecological exams, mammograms. All services provided on a donations-only basis.

Women's Clinic and Family Counseling Center (9911 Pico Blvd., Suite 550, West LA, 310-203-8899) A clean, modern facility with exams done by nurse-practitioners supervised by physicians. Annual exams, screening & treatment for sexually transmitted diseases, ultrasound, mammograms. Also counseling, depression screening, allergy testing and treatment.

Optometric Center of Los Angeles (3916 S. Broadway, LA, 323-234-9137) Clinical facility. Basic eye exam starts at $60, tests and screening for eye diseases, low-cost glasses.

LAC-USC Hospital (1200 N. State St., LA, 323-226-2622) Emergency and trauma care, psychiatric services, neo-natal, general health care.

LA Gay and Lesbian Center (1625 N. Schrader Blvd, Hollywood, 323-993-7400, www.lagaycenter.org) There are SO many services here: a clinic with STD and HIV testing; pap smears; gynecological; mammograms; substance abuse programs. Also transgender, gay and lesbian support groups; mental health counseling; adoption services; anger management; a twenty-four bed homeless youth shelter; adult classes; legal services; etc. Spanish spoken, fees on a sliding scale.

Planned Parenthood LA (Hollywood, Burbank, East LA, Canoga Park, Pomona, Santa Monica, Lawndale, Van Nuys, and Whittier; for a nearby location, call 323-226-0800 or 818-843-2009) STD and HIV testing, prenatal care, family planning, condoms, Norplant, birth control pills, cervical caps, diaphragms, breast exams, male/female sterilizations, hormone therapy, pregnancy tests, emergency contraceptives. Fees are on a sliding scale, Spanish spoken.

MEDICAL MARIJUANA CLINICS

By law in the state of California, those who suffer from HIV/AIDS, cancer, glaucoma, and/or seizures or muscle spasms associated with a chronic, debilitating condition (including epilepsy) qualify for legal access to medical marijuana.

However, if you suffer from any other chronic or persistent medical or psychiatric disorder (e.g., chronic back/neck pain, severe menstrual cramps, depression, anxiety, chronic insomnia, fibromyalgia, social phobia, flight phobia, chronic pain disorder) that either substantially limits your ability to conduct one or more major life activities, and if not alleviated, may cause serious harm to your safety or physical or mental health, you also may qualify for medical marijuana.

How great is that? Go online and find a nearby clinic, make an appointment, bring any current medicine that's been prescribed for your condition and/or your medical records from your doctor, and the clinic's doctor will then write you a "recommendation" for medical marijuana. For first timers, the fee usually ranges from $100 to $175, and recommen-dations need to be renewed yearly, which costs $100.

This recommendation allows you to legally buy your stash over the counter, legally possess it, and legally smoke and be under the influence of it, (keeping in mind, Beevis, not while driving) to ease your pains. The price of medical marijuana varies from $60 to $100, depending on the quality of your purchase.

Visit www.canorml.org/prop/215physicians.html to locate a doctor that will recommend medical marijuana or check out one of the clinics below:

Pacific Support Services (1017 N. La Cienega Blvd., Ste 110, W. Hollywood, 877-GOT-KUSH, PacificSupport Services.com) Tuesday - Thursday 12 pm – 6 pm, walk-ins welcome. $175 for a one-year prescription.

The Holistic Clinic (Every Saturday: Westside Medical Center, 1700 Westwood Blvd. Ste 201, LA. Every Wednesday: Pacific Diagnostics, 9310 East Valley Blvd Ste B, Rosemead. 1-888-420-CLINIC, www.my420clinic.com) By appointment only. $150 for a one-year prescription.

Medical Marijuana of Los Angeles (9663 Santa Monica Blvd, Ste 999, Beverly Hills, 310-923-2626, medicalmarijuana oflosangeles.com) Wednesdays. By appointment only. $100-150 for a one-year prescription.

With a doctor's official recommendation, you can purchase pot legally over the counter at the following dispensaries:

Los Angeles Patients & Caregivers Group, 7213 Santa Monica Blvd., West Hollywood, 323-882-6033, lamedical marijuana.com, Mon – Sat 11 a.m. – 7 p.m., Noon - 7 p.m.

KUSH Collective, 1111 S. La Brea Blvd, LA, 323-938-KUSH, www.lakush.com, Open 11-11 M-Sat.

LA Compassionate Care, 2227 Sunset Blvd., 213-484-1001, 213-272-9489.

Silverlake Caregivers Group, 240 N. Virgil Ave., 213-487-5442. Open M-Sa 10-8.

CRAZY CRYSTAL-WORSHIPPING FREAKS
Well-Being for the Body, Mind and Soul

Yeah, yeah, for years Angelenos have had a rep for being BONKERS with all manner of fads whether it's music, clothing, weirdo cults, plastic surgery or kooky diets. Hell, Tinseltown is loaded (pun intended) with millions of tattooed, salon-tanned, Juicy Couture-clad, red-Kabbalah-string-wearing, newly clean and sober, macrobiotic vegans with a six-figure-per-year shrink habit, biting their super-high-end manicures as they surreptitiously text-message their agent (or personal shopper) from their yoga classes! Still, no matter how completely insane or contradictory some of our behaviors may seem, you gotta admit that, over the years, we had a point with at least *some* of this stuff.

There's a certain amount of stress involved in our big-city lifestyle, even if an inordinately large amount of us have maids, personal assistants, private fitness trainers, an account with a "car service" (i.e., having a limo on call 24/7), stylists, pet therapists, and sober handlers (yes, this is a lucrative job category that actually exists)... not that this book's "target demographic" could afford any of the afore-mentioned but there *are* some ways of alleviating that urban stress by caring for and soothing your rattled brain and bones. And shockingly enough, not only are they healthy, they're affordable!

HEALTHY RESTAURANTS

M CAFE DE CHAYA (7119 Melrose Ave., West Hollywood, 323-525-0588, www.mcafedechaya.com. For delivery: 323-278-3955, www.whycookla.com) This is a bustling, clean café with cuisine based on macrobiotic principles — they use only organic, whole foods — no sugar, eggs, or dairy and everything they make, including the truly decadent desserts (like tiramisu, crème brulee, and mousse cakes) is incredible. They do salad plates, sandwiches, wraps, and sushi among other things. Sunday brunch is a mad house here, but then, where isn't it?

PURAN'S (2064 Hillhurst Ave., Los Feliz, 323-667-1357 or 142 S. La Brea Ave., LA, 323-933-5742) From veggie pizza and salads to grilled chicken; pan-seared scallops to homemade soups, Puran's uses organically-grown produce and herbs and vegetarian-fed, free-range flesh and fowl. Everything is yummy and reasonable here.

VEGETABLE DELIGHT VEGAN CUISINE (17823 Chatsworth, Granada Hills, 818-360-3997) This Asian vegan restaurant is worth the 20-30 drive from LA proper to the North Valley — people have reportedly become addicted!

HEALTH FOOD STORES

EREHWON NATURAL FOODS MART (7660 Beverly Blvd., West Hollywood, 310-937-0777, erehwonmarket.com) This is the granddaddy of health food stores in LA, where you can get anything: fresh organic veggies, cold-pressed oils, vitamins, natural hygiene products. They also have a wonderful café inside the store.

WHOLE FOODS MARKET (7871 Santa Monica Blvd., West Hollywood, 323-848-4200, wholefoodsmarket.com) Erehwon was king until Whole Foods moved in, with locations citywide: Pasadena, Santa Monica, Beverly Hills, Brentwood, etc. This national chain rocks! We're talking 50-cent liters of water, fresh flowers, aisles of natural skin care products and cosmetics, vitamins, homeopathic remedies, fitness DVDs, bulk nuts, recycled cards and giftwrap. Their deli is astounding and vast, and the servers are always very liberal with free samples. The West Hollywood location is renowned for having a cute staff and customers (think hard bodies, rainbow dreads, tattoos and piercings), and is known throughout LA as a prime pick-up spot to boot.

FUN WAYS TO SWEAT

HOLLYWOOD YMCA (1553 Schrader, Hollywood, 323-467-4161, www.ymcala.org) They offer all sorts of classes from dance and yoga to martial arts and aquatics, racquetball courts, personal trainers — not to mention daycare, counseling, a transitional living facility for women, and even financial aid for membership. The **Downtown Ketchum YMCA** (401 S.

Hope, Downtown LA, 213-624-0548) is great, too, with more of the same.

GOLDEN BRIDGE YOGA (6322 De Longpre, Hollywood, 323-936-4172, www.goldenbridgeyoga.com) You can always see some starlets slurping smoothies in the lobby here, and the work wear and gift items in the store are a bit on the pricey side, but this facility offers all manner of yoga, from pre-natal to kundalini, plus meditation, Sufi rituals, African dance, chanting, and sometimes they feature concerts, lectures and poetry readings at night.

SILVER LAKE YOGA (2810 1/2 Glendale Blvd., Silver Lake, 323- 953-0496, silverlakeyoga.com) Isn't quite as hoity-toity as Golden Bridge, (which means the celeb-sighting quotient isn't as high) but they offer all levels of classes all day, including pre-natal and yoga for toddlers.

PILATES WESTWOOD (1309 Westwood Blvd., West LA, 310-914-1796, www.westwoodpilates.com) They offer private and semi-private Pilates instruction at reasonable rates.

GODDESS LIFE CENTER (4051 Glencoe Ave., Marina Del Rey, 310-281-7427, goddesslife.com) This ain't your mama's dance studio! Run by the vivacious Dolphina, (of the *Goddess Workout* DVD series), Goddess Life features regular bellydance classes, evening candlelight classes, full moon rituals, even lap dancing and cheerleading workshops!

BELLY DANCE LA (www.bellydancela.com) This comprehensive website run by dancer Dannette Riddle has a weekly and monthly calendar with info on bellydance classes all over Los Angeles and Orange Counties, special events and show listings, plus many informative articles on bellydance and Arabic culture.

MASSAGE/SPA SERVICES

HEALING HANDS WELLNESS CENTER (417 N. Larchmont Blvd., LA, 323-461-7686, www.healing handswc.com) Okay, I have this place on speed-dial: they have wonderful massages that are $55 for an hour, $75 for 90 minutes, in a clean, tranquil environment... and they're open seven days *and* take walk-ins! They also have acupuncture and chiropractic services. Healing Hands is located in Larchmont Village, a quaint couple of pleasant blocks in the midst of Hollywood, with many cute cafes, bookstores, boutiques, and cosmetics emporium/salon/spas.

LARCHMONT BEAUTY CENTER (208 N. Larchmont, LA, 323-461-0162) within stumbling distance. Larchmont Beauty not only stocks a mind-boggling selection of cosmetics, hair products, nailcare items, accessories, jewelry and personal care products, they have a full service spa and salon offering everything from facials and waxing to massage.

BURKE WILLIAMS (www.burkewilliamsspa.com) With locations all over LA, including West LA, Sherman Oaks and Pasadena, this chain offers many different massage and beauty treatments (facials, body wraps) as well as packages, all at affordable prices. The West Hollywood branch (8000 Sunset Blvd) is also practically next door to the Virgin Megastore, many eateries, and some nifty shops.

THE CENTER FOR WELLBEING (75 N. Baldwin Ave., Sierra Madre, CA 91024, 626-355-2443) From Swedish to Shiatsu-amma to heated stone massage, they've got it all and more: spa facials, European facials, reflexology, hydrating treatments, waxing, microdermabrasion. Ask for Yvonne, her hands are *magic*. Located about half an hour east of LA proper, it's not too far to drive, and they will also send therapists to private homes, offices, and film sets for an nominal extra fee, based on distance.

ALTERNATIVE MEDICINE

AMERICAN UNIVERSITY OF COMPLIMENTARY MEDICINE (11543 Olympic Blvd., LA, 310-914-4116, www.auc.org) This umbrella school of world medicine features homeopathy, Ayurvedic and Chinese Classical medicine, as well as holistic herbology, nutritional medicine and the like. They offer certifications in the various practices, while at the same time serving the community for reduced rates.

DR. WILSON PARK, D.C., C.C.F.C AND WEST LA PILATES (2940 Westwood Blvd., West LA, 90064, 310-869-0536, www.westlapilates.com) Tucked away in a post-WWII, total *Leave It To Beaver* neighborhood is this little jewel of a full-service healing center. Dr. Park is not only a great chiropractor, he does bio-mechanics and almost super-human injury rehabilitation. His client list includes Olympic athletes and world-class dancers, as well as average folks suffering from repetitive stress injuries. He restored my complete range of motion due to severe tendonitis in both wrists, which left me pain-free. He's the only doctor I've ever been to that takes time to give personalized treatment, answer questions in detail, gives therapeutic "homework" exercises *and* will keep you entertained by chatting about everything from the paranormal to the latest plot turns on *Desperate Housewives*! Also offered here are phenomenal one-on-one Pilates instruction by Patte

James, acupuncture, massage, and there is a nutritionist on staff.

MIND
THE BODHI TREE BOOKSTORE AND ANNEX (8583-8585 Melrose Ave., West Hollywood, 310-659-1733, www.bodhitree.com) The Bodhi Tree has been serving LA since 1970. In fact, it was New Age when New Age wasn't cool! The store is *the* place for books on philosophy, the paranormal, Eastern religions, alternative treatments, ad infinitum... plus gifts, CDs, and DVDs. They hold events like readings, booksignings and lectures often, and publish *Evolve* magazine. In the Annex, there are astrologers, Tarot readers, Reiki healers, and numerologists. Come here for a consultation, reading or class. Across the street they run **Elixir Teas and Tonics**, (8612 Melrose, 310- 657-9310) which serves raw food treats and great natural bevvies.

HYPNOSIS MOTIVATION INSTITUTE (18607 Ventura Blvd., Suite 310, Tarzana, 818-758-2747, www.hypnosis.edu) Quit smoking, stop biting your nails, overcome a childhood trauma through hypnosis... or get certified as a hypnotherapist yourself! Since 1968, the non-profit, nationally accredited Hypnosis Motivation Institute offers programs and classes in hypnosis, neuro-linguistic programming, and therapeutic imagery. You're getting sleepy...

SOUL
HARE KRISHNA TEMPLE LOS ANGELES (305 Rose Ave., Venice, 310-450-5371) Forget the Blue Man Group, there's only one blue man here and of course, it's Krishna! Come for study, worship, meditation... or just to buy cool ethnic threads and chow down at **Radha Govinda's**, their marvelous

veggie-cuisine café. Every summer, they also sponsor the **Festival of the Chariots** at Venice beach, complete with painted, flower-bedecked elephants on parade, live music, lots of chanting and a free Indian feast for everyone.

SAN FERNANDO VALLEY HONGWANJI BUDDHIST TEMPLE (9450 Remick Ave., Pacoima) Om is where the heart is.... Meditate, contemplate and get in the zen!

SINAI TEMPLE (10400 Wilshire Blvd., LA, 310-474-1518, www.sinaitemple.org) This is the place that makes Judaism fun... and you don't have to worry about Madonna and Guy Ritchie showing up with an entourage! Rabbi David Wolpe is young and hip without losing his religion to Hollywood aspirations. In addition to services and Hebrew classes, Sinai also has guest speakers, story-hour for tots, seminars like "Spirituality For Super Moms," and the hands-down favorite, "Friday Night Live" which offers a Shabbat unlike any other, featuring live music and a Middle Eastern buffet. It usually attracts crowds of up to 1,500 though, so get there early!

ISLAMIC CENTER OF SOUTHERN CALIFORNIA (434 S. Vermont Ave., LA, 213-384-5783, www.internetmuslim.org) Here you can find out what Islam is really about — they offer worship, study, and community outreach.

HOLLYWOOD UNITED METHODIST CHURCH (6817 Franklin Ave., Hollywood, 323-874-2104, hollywoodumc.org) Just down the street from the Hollywood Bowl (and they offer Bowl parking, too!) is this huge, great church. In fact, you may have seen it in flicks like *Sister Act* or *Jarhead.* They have worship services, daycare, community outreach, an AIDS ministry, a huge gym and rentable reception hall.

LA ON FOUR LEGS

Here are some good resources for pet owners in Los Angeles:

ANIMAL SURGICAL AND EMERGENCY CENTER
(1535 Sepulveda, near Santa Monica Blvd., West LA, 310-473-1561, 24 Hours) This awesome hospital not only offers around-the-clock emergency care, they also have vets that keep regular office hours. But this isn't just an animal ER, they have specialists and miracle-working surgeons that go above and beyond treatment at a neighborhood animal hospital. They saved my kitty, Beigey–Brown, who had a collapsed lung, among other complications. Okay, so it wasn't cheap... but five and a half years later, she's running around like it never happened. I still think it was the best "purr-chase" I ever made!

ANIMAL EMERGENCY CENTER (11730 Ventura Blvd., Studio City, 818-760-3882, 5 p.m. - 8:30 a.m. weeknights, and 24 hours on weekends) This small hospital has a caring staff of vets available to treat "after-hours" animal emergencies, from simple mishaps to major accidents.

VETERINARY MEDICAL CENTER (11723 Ventura Blvd., Studio City, 818-762-3111, www.veterinarymedical center.com) Dr. Steve Aboulafia and the staff of VMC are friendly and compassionate, taking care of everything from shots and check-ups to surgery. They offer feline and canine dental care, spaying, neutering, boarding, and several lines of restricted diet specialty foods. Charlie, the feline answer to George Clooney on *ER* is a foxy white kitty with a bedside manner (and the run of the place) that lounges on top of the admissions desk, checking out the incoming patients.

GATEWAY ANIMAL HOSPITAL (431 W. Los Feliz Blvd., LA, 323-256- 5840) A small full-service hospital which takes city-sponsored spaying and neutering coupons. Routine office visits start at $38.

VETMOBILE (310-412-7000) This is *not* an emergency service. You need to make an appointment in advance, but they will take your pet to the doctor when you can't.

FIFI AND ROMEO (7282 Beverly Boulevard, W. Hollywood, 323-857-7215 www.fifiandromeo.com) This is like a fashionista store for critters: a whimsical, frivolous pet accessories store. Need a rhinestone collar, a doggie sweater, or gourmet treats?

TAIL WAGGERS (1929 N. Bronson Ave., Hollywood, 323-464-9600, www.twaggers.com) A small, friendly high-end pet store located in the Hollywood foothills. Friendly, informative staff, and everything from food, collars and leashes to organic home-made dog biscuits, pet books, artsy food bowls, etc.

TAIL WASHERS (1927 N. Bronson Ave., Hollywood, 323-464-9600, www.twaggers.com) Run by Tailwaggers, this brand new facility is located just next door. They offer self-washing, but also have professional groomers on hand.

PETCO (locations all over Los Angeles, www.petco.com) Open seven days: pet supplies and food, aquariums and fish, birds, small reptiles, varying by location. They are usually inexpensive and most locations offer bulk pet chow and dog biscuits, too. Some stores offer grooming and vaccination clinics once a month, or a few times a year.

BRONSON CANYON PARK (Bronson Ave., north of Franklin, Hollywood, park closes at sunset) Drive up past the picnic tables to the last parking lot. Park your car; grab a leash for Rover, and head to your left, up the dirt road. A few feet along, you can let your doggie off the leash (like everyone else does... technically, you're not supposed to) and hike through the canyon until you get up to the Bat Caves. Yup, this crazy rock formation of three cave-like tunnels is the real location of the exterior of the Bat Cave from 1960s TV series *Bat Man*. It's also been featured in a ton of movies, everything from early "B" Westerns to *Short Cuts*. Dogs love sniffing around up here. Even if you don't have a dog, you will, too.

AUTO EROTIC

Everything you've heard about a car being an absolute necessity in Los Angeles is true. Over the past few years, there have been many improvements in public transportation, but having wheels at your disposal will make your life *much* easier. If you're not used to driving in LA, you should know that all of those clichés and horror stories are true as well. Traffic is consistently insane: LA drivers eat, babble on cell phones, apply make-up, flirt with other drivers, blow red lights, make u-turns at random, and barely ever bother to signal. As far as most people are concerned, a yellow light means "Drive as fast as you can." Be forewarned, all you wannabe street-rodders: many intersections have those infamous cameras that will photograph you cruising through an intersection, and then send you an astronomical ticket. Gridlock and road rage are a fact of everyday life. But gruesome as it may sound, there are days when traffic flows smoothly, it's sunny, you're on your way to the beach, and driving in LA is great.

Word to the wise: read posted signs *carefully* before parking! The notorious Parking Enforcement assholes (job requirements are, in no particular order: having a scary hair-do, a big fat butt, and a bad attitude) would like nothing better than to give you a ticket. Sometimes paying an exorbitant valet parking fee may be more financially sound than driving around looking for a space on the street.

Also, in California, car insurance is mandatory. Your license could be suspended if you don't have it. And it's probably a good idea to join the **AAA Auto Club** (various locations in Southern California, www.aaa-calif.com). They'll bring you gas, jump-start your car, and provide four free tows a year if you get stranded someplace. They also offer car insurance, and if you're a member, you can get perks like safety check-ups, driving directions, and discounts to hotels, car rentals, and tourist attractions.

Always remember to lock your car, and *never* leave anything valuable in it. LA always has been — and always will be — a place that worships at the Altar of the Auto, so here are some places that'll help you feel the love:

CAR RENTAL
FLEXCAR (various locations, 877-FLEXCAR, flexcar.com)
  Rent by the hour, membership fee required. Gas + insurance
  included in price.
AVIS (various locations, 800-831-2847, www.avis.com)
BUDGET (various locations, 800-527-0700, budget.com)
ENTERPRISE (free customer pick-up and returns, various
  locations, 800-325-8007, www.enterprise.com)
HERTZ (free customer pick-up and returns, various locations,
  800-704-4473, www.hertz.com)

AUTO PARTS AND ACCESSORIES

KRAGEN (Citywide, many locations, www.kragen.com)

AUTO ZONE (Citywide, many locations, autozone.com) A great place to go for new parts and tools if you do home repairs, or to pick up oil, transmission fluid, car wax, etc.

Another store that has multiple locations belongs to **Manny, Moe and Jack** — made famous by LA punk band, The Dickies — and officially known as **PEP BOYS** (many locations citywide, www.pepboys.com)

REPAIR

HOLLYWOOD SPRING AND AXEL (6009 W. Sunset, Hollywood, 323-464-4051) This place looks like a set from *The Fast and the Furious,* a true old-school garage. There are engines, tires and vintage auto hulks lying around, a (friendly) pit bull on a chain, and grease-stained pin-ups of racecars and foxy chicks lining the walls. Honest, fast, inexpensive service, and gearhead extraordinaire maniac/mechanic Chris Doyle is GOD. Really. I actually got on my hands and knees and kow-towed to him in the middle of the street once, because he has saved my ass — and my '64 Comet Caliente — so many times.

THOMAS TOPS (1317 Caheunga Blvd., Hollywood, 323-469-3277) If you need to get a convertible roof redone, this is the place to go. They also do auto interiors, car covers, and even boats. They are reliable and work quickly.

JERRY'S GARAGE (1645 N. Gower, Hollywood, 323-464-7381) A small, all-service garage that does routine maintenance and major repairs on everything from domestic and foreign cars to news vans. Honest, affordable work and the staff are all nice people.

FUN STUFF

PETERSON AUTO MUSEUM (6060 Wilshire Blvd., LA, 323-930-CARS, www.petersen.org) the museum features cars as art. Past shows have included movie vehicles, souped-up hot rods, vintage autos, and wildly decorated custom Low Rider cars.

DREAM BOATS (12333 W. Pico Blvd., LA, 310-828-3014) The place to go if you wanna make like a movie star and rent some styley wheels (like a cherried out '30s gangster sedan or '57 Chevy convertible) for a special occasion. Starting at $89 a day, it isn't cheap, but if you got the dough, go for it.

THE BLESSING OF THE CARS (www.blessingof thecars.com) If you like cars and you happen to be in the LA area during the last week of July, you *must* attend this bash, your mind will be blown. Run by the ultra-hip husband and wife team Gabriel and Stephanie Baltierra, BOTC is an annual all-day event, which features a vintage car and motorcycle show, contests with prizes for things like "Best Flames" and "Best Street Rod." There are booths with auto accessories, new and used parts, specialty car magazines and books, car-themed T-shirts, and food. People-watching is prime too, with a bunch of cute grease monkeys and Bettie Page clones running around showing off their tattoos in skimpy sundresses. Bands play all day long, there's usually a pin-striping or detailing demonstration, auto-themed art, and '50s hot rod movies being screened. Oh, and of course there's a Catholic priest on hand (dressed in checkered, racing-striped vestments) to bless your vehicle.

POMONA AUTO SWAPMEET (Every six weeks on Sunday, from 5 a.m. - 2 p.m., Los Angeles County Fairplex, 1101 W. McKinley, Pomona, 909-623-3711, pomonaswapmeet.com) You won't believe this swap meet. It stretches almost as far as the eye can see. Dealers from all over California and neighboring states bring cars to buy and sell. From perfectly restored vintage vehicles to frightening clunkers, from seats to upholstery buttons, nitro-blasting hot-rods to Model-Ts, as well as the odd Airstream trailer, dirt bikes, kiddie toy cars, motorcycles, old racing trophies, antique Schwinn bicycles, auto magazines, racing leathers, T-shirts, coveralls, chrome parts and logos, you name it. Dreaming of a fully restored 1932 Highboy or a lime green metal flake pimpmobile with a faux-fur interior and the signs of the zodiac decorating the steering wheel? If you can't find it here, it probably doesn't exist. Bargaining is a must. Make sure to bring sunblock, water, and cold, hard cash. If you're looking for a used car and don't feel like waiting for the swap meet, check out **www.craiglist.com** or pick up a copy of *The Recycler* or *Photo Buys* (both available at newsstands and convenience stores, every Thursday) or try your luck with the extensive used auto listings.

ANNUAL PARTIES and CITYWIDE EVENTS

LA goes all-out to celebrate holidays, whether they are tradition-based or just an excuse to have a great time. This is by no means a complete list, but certain yearly events are tons of fun, and many are free. Here are a few of the better ones:

JANUARY
THE TOURNAMENT OF THE ROSES PARADE (Pasadena citywide, 626-441-3150 or 626-449-4100, www.tournamentofroses.com) New Year's Day. Amazing to see — and smell — in real life. All the floats are made out of flowers. Standing or sitting in the street is free, but the good

spots fill up the night before: prepare to camp out. The floats are also on display to see up close 'n' personal for the next week or so, at the end of the parade route.

FEBRUARY

AFRICAN-AMERICAN HISTORY MONTH (323-295-0521 for info, locations, and schedule) Citywide celebrations.

CHINESE NEW YEAR CELEBRATION (North Broadway, near Spring St., Chinatown, 323-617-0396 ext.13, www.lagoldendragonparade.com) The amazing and traditional Golden Dragon Parade is a central event in the celebration of Chinese New Year, which also includes a carnival, crafts, food, a Mah Jong tournament, Tai Chi workshops, and, of course, the LA Miss Chinatown Contest.

MARCH

THE BLESSING OF THE ANIMALS (125 Paseo de la Plaza and El Pueblo de Los Angeles, Downtown LA, 323-628-7164) Total pandemonium (and lots of flying fur and over-dressed pooches) as people flock to this free event to get their pets — including cats and dogs, ducks, parrots, horses, iguanas, turtles, *whatever* — blessed by Catholic priests.

THE LA MARATHON (310-444-5544) This 26-mile course is great for the runners and cyclists, but if you're trying to go anywhere before 4 p.m., FORGET IT! Free to all who wish to watch. Along the route, the LA Cacophony Society (a group of creative jokesters) delight in offering a "pit-stop" for runners featuring cheeseburgers and candy bars, beer, cigarettes, and lap dances! It's street theater at its finest.

APRIL

EARTH DAY (www.earthday.net) Check local listings for many activities and volunteer opportunities — such as pitching in to clean up local parks and beaches.

FESTIVAL DE LOS NINOS (Caesar Chavez and Soto St., East LA, 818-734-2744) The Latin community celebrates kids and springtime with this festival, featuring Hispanic foods, crafts, a fun fair with rides and more.

LA INDEPENDENT FILM FESTIVAL (Citywide, 310-289-2000) put on by the Directors Guild of America, this festival features the best of independent films from established and emerging directors.

MAY

CINCO DE MAYO (El Pueblo de Los Angeles and Olvera St., downtown LA) Aztec dancers, food, live music, crafts all focused on cultural heritage than Fiesta Broadway. Also check local papers for neighborhood festivals. Words to the wise: please don't drink and drive!

JUNE

CAIRO CARNIVALE (Santa Anita Racetrack, Arcadia, 818-503-2511, www.mecda.org) A fantastic festival put on by the Middle Eastern Culture And Dance Association (MECDA) Cairo Carnival celebrates the dancing of the Middle East, North Africa, and Mediterranean, with dancers from all over California performing non-stop. Also live drummers, dance classes, a Gypsy camp, magicians, sword-swallowers, Middle Eastern food, charity raffles and contests, face-painting, dance costumes and instruments for sale. Tons of fun!

GAY AND LESBIAN, TRANSGENDER PRIDE
(Christopher St. West and West Hollywood Park, 323-860-0701, www.lapride.org) An amazing parade full of drag cheerleading squads and the awesome Dykes on Bikes, a carnival, info booths, bands, and a city full of queer and queer-friendly folks celebrating like mad. Usually the third weekend in June.

JULY
FOURTH OF JULY FIREWORKS DISPLAYS (323-881-2411 for citywide info)

SANTA MONICA PIER TWILIGHT DANCE (Ocean and Colorado, Santa Monica, 310-458-8900, www.santa monicapier.com) For years, every summer on balmy Thursday evenings, there are free concerts on the Pier, and it's awesome, duuuude! From Brazilian to country, rock, jazz, etc. Name artists perform for free. Have some cotton candy, snuggle your honey and watch the sun set.

THE LOTUS FESTIVAL (Echo Park Lake, Downtown LA, 323-485-8744, www.lacity.org) Celebrate Asian/Pacific Rim cultures with dragonboat races, a flower show, ethnic food, kids' activities, various shows of music and dance.

THE BLESSING OF THE CARS (www.myspace.com/blessingofthecars) Put on by husband and wife Gabriel and Stephanie Baltierra, this always takes place on the last weekend of July. Hot rods and classic cars on display, there's a priest on hand to bless your ride, a car-themed art show, car accessories, clothes and hot rod stuff for sale, food, live rockabilly and swing bands, and of course, hot trophy girls!

AUGUST

AFRICAN MARKETPLACE AND CULTURAL FAIR
(Exposition Park, Crenshaw District, www.lacity.org) Music, dancing, mask-making, African-American crafts, yummy food, clothing booths, fortune-telling, hair-weaving, live entertainment.

WATTS SUMMER FESTIVAL (Watts, 323-789-7304, www.wattsfestival.org) A weeklong festival with art exhibits, crafts, food booths, community information, and sports.

SEPTEMBER

LA COUNTY FAIR (Pomona Sportsplex, 909-623-3111, www.lacountyfair.com) Definitely worth the 40-minute drive and reasonable admission, this is the world's largest county fair with rides, shows, bands, games, kiddie stuff, tons of food and livestock. See pigs bigger than your sofa! Eat cotton candy! Squaredance!

OCTOBER

AFI FILM FESTIVAL (Citywide, 323-466-1767, www.afifest.com) One of the biggest film festivals in the US.

WEST HOLLYWOOD HALLOWEEN CELEBRATION
(Santa Monica Blvd., between La Cienega and Doheny, 310-848-6308) This takes up practically the whole neighborhood. Witness drunk done-to-the-nines drag queens, impromptu performances, mobbed bars, scary people doing scary things... tons o' fun and free, which means there's a high tourist gawk-factor. You practically have to sell your soul to Satan to get a parking space within miles of this event, but it's worth it! Wear flat shoes if possible because, girrrrrl, you're going to walk... a lot.

NOVEMBER

DIA DE LOS MUERTOS (ladayofthedead.com) Dia de los Muertos is a big deal here in Los Angeles, and there are celebrations everywhere. Two of the best are on Olvera Street, also known as El Pueblo De Los Angeles, where you can buy traditional sugar skulls, watch Aztec dancers, dress up like a skeleton, eat Mexican food, and swig Tecate and cheap margaritas. **Hollywood Forever Memorial Park** (6000 Santa Monica Blvd., Hollywood, hollywoodforever.com) also does a bang-up version of this Mexican holiday where, traditionally, families would honor their dead by cleaning the graves and picnicking among the headstones or mausoleums. Hollywood Forever hosts many local artisans, who do elaborate Dia de los Muertos installations inside the cemetery. There are also ballet folklorico groups, live music, crafts for sale, and of course, you can visit the graves of the famous people interred here, including Jayne Mansfield, Mel Blanc, Tyrone Power, Rudolph Valentino, and the many Armenian mobsters who have grave markers bigger than any of the aforementioned stars.

HOLLYWOOD CHRISTMAS PARADE (Hollywood and Sunset Boulevards closed between Bronson and La Brea, Thanksgiving Weekend Sunday, parade usually starts about 5 p.m., www.hollywoodchamberofcommerce.net) Floats, celebrities, marching bands from all over the country, fancy Western equestrian teams, the Budweiser Clydesdales, and Santa. Also a lot of street vendors, inebriated trailer trash, Scientologists giving free personality tests among the crowd, gangbangers, and bag people, plus a ton of third-rate, z-list celebs that *nobody* recognizes waving from the most of the floats... but always fun. Dress warmly, the event usually lasts over two hours and it does get cold. For the best curbside seating, camp out mid-afternoon, and bring a thermos of something toasty to drink.

DECEMBER

DOWNTOWN ON ICE (Pershing Square, Downtown, 818-243-6488) Late November through January. Yes, it's just like skating Rockefeller Center... well, sort of. This outdoor ice rink has been pleasing winter-wannabe's for years. They even rent skates!

GRIFFITH PARK LIGHT FESTIVAL (Crystal Springs Rd., Griffith Park, 213-485-8743, www.dwplightfestival.com, lit between 5-10 p.m. before Christmas) This really is spectacular... like a winter wonderland without the snow... no, makes that a fairyland. There's a full mile of Christmas light displays, depicting everything from reindeer and elves to patriotic themes. Be prepared to sit waiting with your engine idling for at least 45 minutes if you go there early: that's when all the family cars packed full of kiddies show up and it's a madhouse. Lotsa people admiring the displays with, uh, bloodshot eyes, too!

LA THEME PARKS and ATTRACTIONS

Call ahead to confirm hours and admission prices!

KNOTT'S BERRY FARM (8039 Beach Blvd., Buena Park, 714-220-5200, www.knotts.com) Open daily except Christmas. Knott's has six areas of exciting rides, live shows, and restaurants, most based on a Wild West theme. They also provide a shuttle from major LA area hotels and offer discounted group rates for 15 or more. Tickets: general admission $39.95, seniors (over 62) $14.95, children (3-11) $14.95, and children under 2 are free.

SIX FLAGS CALIFORNIA: MAGIC MOUNTAIN AND HURRICANE HARBOR (Interstate 5, Valencia, 818-367-5965, sixflags.com) Located about 40 minutes north of LA, Magic Mountain offers a one-price admission for heart-pounding thrill rides, spine-cracking coasters, concerts, shows, and attractions. Next door is **Hurricane Harbor Waterpark**

(open May - September) - separate admission required. **Six Flags** opens daily at 10 a.m. during the extended summer months, and weekends and holidays the rest of the year. Tickets: general admission $59.99, children $29.99, and children under 2 are free.

DISNEYLAND (Anaheim, 714-781-7290, www.disney land.com) Mickey Mouse as far as the eye can see. Located about 30 minutes south of downtown LA, Disneyland is the granddaddy of theme parks, spread out over 65 acres with a resort hotel complex. Kiddie rides, thrill rides, live shows, fireworks, roving characters, movies, and virtual attractions, plus guided tours. Open everyday. Hours are generally 10 a.m. to 10 p.m., but may vary so call ahead. Locals know that the park is generally a lot less crowded on overcast, chilly, or rainy days, and this really makes a difference in the time you spend waiting in line, so you might want to take that into consideration when you plan your trip. Disneyland does not sell tickets, they sell "passports": regular $45, children (3-9) $35, and children under 3 are free. California residents (with ID) get in for $35 and seniors for $43. Longer passport rates for multiple entry are available, too. Disneyland has an entire new adjacent park open as well, called *Disney's California Adventure*. Admission is separate (same as Disneyland rates) and all the rides, attractions and shows have a California theme. (Editors' note: Don't even think of trying to pose with one of the characters while giving "the finger," you'll get arrested every time).

SEA WORLD (500 Sea World Dr., San Diego, 714-939-6212. Directions: 619-226-3901, seaworld.com) From Interstate 5 or 8, exit Seaworld Drive and turn west towards the park entrance. Open daily at 10 a.m. (9 during summer). Aquariums, an outdoor stadium with sharks, seals, dolphins, killer whales, polar bears, and more; including Baby Shamu, born in 2001. Five different shows, twenty attractions and exhibits, plus gift shops and a number of restaurants. Single day tickets: adult $53 children (ages 3-9) $43. Multi-day passes also available.

UNIVERSAL STUDIOS CITY WALK AND TOUR (100 Universal City Plaza, Universal City, 818-622-3801, www.universalstudios.com, weekdays 10 a.m. - 6 p.m., 9 a.m. – 6 p.m. weekends) The City Walk has theme-based restaurants, including all things sausage, a beachy fish place, B.B. King's Blues Club, a magic eatery, etc.; a huge megaplex movie theater; the Universal Amphitheater, which features everything from rock to the Radio City Music Hall Rockettes, and tons of stores. The Tour's tram winds through the studio's back lot: see King Kong up close, the *Jaws* shark, the house from *Psycho*, a Spiderman and more. Also, movie-themed thrill rides: *E.T.*, *Shrek*, and *Jurassic Park* (bring yer raincoat for that last one!) Interactive shows, street performers, and celeb impersonators for photo-ops. Single day tickets: general admission $59, children under 3 are free.

NBC STUDIOS TOUR (3000 W. Alameda, Burbank, 818-840-3537, www.seeing-stars.coml) Not exactly a theme park, but it's the only television network that gives guided tours and it's ten minutes away from central Hollywood. Visit the *Tonight Show* set, see the sound, special effects, and wardrobe departments, and maybe even get a glimpse of a star! You can also request free *Tonight Show* tickets, available on a first-come, first-served basis, or write ahead and specify the day you wish to be part of the audience.

HOLLYWOOD WAX MUSEUM (6767 Hollywood Blvd., Hollywood, 323-462-8860 hollywoodwax.com) Open daily from 10 till midnight, and until 1 a.m. on weekends. This slightly cheesy extravaganza features everything from "The Last Supper" to *The Wizard of Oz*, plus all your fave Hollywood stars, old and new. Adults: $12.95, seniors: $8.50, kids 6-12: $6.95, under six, free. It's also located only about a block from...

GRAUMAN'S CHINESE THEATRE (6915 Hollywood Blvd., Hollywood, manntheatres.com/chinese) where, for free, you can browse around the courtyard and fit your feet into the footprints of Clark Gable, Marilyn Monroe, the Marx Brothers... heck, even the cast of *Baywatch*! This is also the place to catch various bus tour vans for guided tours through Hollywood — and how could you miss the mega-mall at Hollywood and Highland, featuring clubs, restaurants, and the brand new home of the Oscars, the Kodak Theater.

RIPLEY'S BELIEVE IT OR NOT MUSEUM (6780 Hollywood Blvd., Hollywood, 323-466-6335, ripleys.com) This gem of modern schlock features curiosities ranging from strange to mind-boggling. See a life-sized statue of John Wayne made out of laundry lint, two-headed calves, and real shrunken heads. Adults: $11.95, kids 6-12 $7.95 (5 and under free) and discounts of a dollar off admissions for seniors, military personnel and AAA members.

GUINNESS BOOK OF WORLD RECORDS MUSEUM (6764 Hollywood Blvd., Hollywood, 323-463-6433) More tacky fun discovering the shortest, tallest, fastest, loudest, richest, most tattooed, etc. Crazy facts about humans, natural disasters, science, literature, show business, you name it. Adults: $11.95, seniors: $7.95, kids 5-12: $6.95, under 4: free.

MUSEUMS

** Free once a month or everyday
* Cheap (under $5) admission

THE AUTRY MUSEUM OF WESTERN HERITAGE
(4700 Western Heritage Way, Griffith Park, 323-667-2000,
www.autry-museum.org) Closed Monday, open 10 a.m. - 5
p.m.; $7.50, $5 seniors & students, $3 children ages 2 to 12,
under 2 free.

*CABRILLO MARINE AQUARIUM** (3720 Stephen White
Dr., San Pedro, 310-548-7562, www.cabrilloaq.org) Open
Tues. - Fri. noon - 5 p.m., Sat. - Sun. 10 a.m. - 5 p.m., $2
suggested donation for adults, $1 children & seniors.

CALIFORNIA AFRICAN-AMERICAN MUSEUM (600
State Dr., Exposition Park, 213-744-7432, caamuseum.org)
Open Wed. - Sat., 10 a.m. - 4 p.m., free.

**CALIFORNIA SCIENCE CENTER (700 State Dr., Exposition Park, 213-744-7400, california sciencecenter.org) Open daily, 10 a.m. - 5 p.m., free. Formerly the Museum of Science and Industry.

**GETTY CENTER (1200 Getty Center Dr., West LA, 310-440-7300, www.getty.edu) Open Sat.- Sun. 10 a.m. - 6 p.m., Tues.- Wed. 11 a.m. - 7 p.m., Thurs.- Fri. 11 a.m. - 9 p.m., free. Parking is $7 and reservations are required.

*GRIER MUSSER ANTIQUES MUSEUM (403 S. Bonnie Brae St., 213-413-1814, griermusser museum.com) Wed. - Fri. noon - 4 p.m., Sat. 11 a.m. - 4 p.m., $7 adults, $4 children & seniors. Call ahead.

HOLLYWOOD ENTERTAINMENT MUSEUM (7021 Hollywood Blvd., 323-465-7900, hollywoodmuseum.com) Closed Wednesdays, daily 11 a.m. - 6 p.m., $12, $5 seniors and children, under 5 free.

**HUNTINGTON LIBRARY, ART COLLECTIONS, AND BOTANICAL GARDENS (1151 Oxford Road, San Marino, 626-405-2141, www.huntington.org) Open Tues. - Fri. noon - 4:30 p.m., Sat. - Sun., 10:30 a.m. - 4:30 p.m., $15, $12.50 seniors, $10 students, $6 children 5-11, under 4 free. Free admission the first Thursday of every month.

JAPANESE AMERICAN NATIONAL MUSEUM (369 E. First St., 213-625-0414, www.janm.org) Open Tues. - Sun. 10 a.m. - 5 p.m., Thurs. 10 a.m. - 8 p.m. (free 5 p.m. - 8 p.m.), $8, $5 seniors, $4 students & free for members & children over 5.

**KOREAN CULTURAL CENTER (5505 Wilshire Blvd., 323-936-7141, www.kccla.org) Open Mon. - Fri. 9 a.m. - 5 p.m., Sat. 10 a.m. - 1 p.m., free.

LOS ANGELES CHILDREN'S MUSEUM (Scheduled to open 2007, childrensmuseumla.org)

**LOS ANGELES COUNTY MUSEUM OF ART (5905 Wilshire Blvd., 323-857-6000, www.lacma.org) Open Mon., Tues. & Thurs., noon - 8 p.m., Fri. noon - 9 p.m., Sat. - Sun. 11 a.m. - 8 p.m., $9, $5 students & seniors over 62, children 17 and under free. Free admission the second Tuesday of every month.

**MUSEUM OF CONTEMPORARY ART (250 S. Grand Ave., 213-626-6222, www.moca-la.org) Mon. 11 a.m. – 5 p.m., Tues. & Wed. closed, Thurs. 11 a.m. – 8 p.m. (5 p.m. – 8 p.m. free), Fri. 11 a.m. – 5 p.m., Saturday 11 a.m. – 6 p.m. Sun. 11 a.m. – 6 p.m., $8, $5 seniors & students, members & children under 12 free. Free admission every Thurs. 5 p.m. - 8 p.m.

**MUSEUM OF JURASSIC TECHNOLOGY (9341 Venice Blvd., West LA, 310-836-6131, www.mjt.org) Thursdays from 2 p.m. - 8 p.m., Fri, Sat. & Sun. noon - 6 p.m., $5, $3 seniors, students, and children 12 to 21, $2 disabled, $3 unemployed, under 12, free.

*MUSEUM OF LATIN AMERICAN ART (628 Alamitos Ave., Long Beach, 562-437-1689, www.molaa.com) Open Tues. - Fri., 11:30 a.m. - 7:00 p.m., Sat. 11 a.m. - 7 p.m., Sun. 11 a.m. - 6 p.m., $5, $3 seniors, children under 12 free.

**MUSEUM OF NEON ART/MONA (501 W. Olympic at Hope St., 213-489-9918, www.neonmona.org) Open Wed. - Sat. 11 a.m. - 5 p.m., Sun. noon - 5 p.m., $5, $3.50 students & seniors, children under 13 free. Free 2nd Thursday evening of every month.

MUSEUM OF TELEVISION AND RADIO (465 N. Beverly Dr., Beverly Hills, 310-786-1000, www.mtr.org) Open Wed. - Sun. noon - 5 p.m., free.

MUSEUM OF TOLERANCE (9786 W. Pico Blvd., 310-553-9036, www.museumoftolerance.com) Open Mon. - Thurs. 11 a.m. - 4 p.m.; Fri. 11 a.m. - 3 p.m., Sun., 11 a.m. - 5 p.m., closed Saturday. Tours take approximately 2 hours and reservations are recommended. $10, $8 seniors 62 & up, $7 students and children.

**NATURAL HISTORY MUSEUM (900 Exposition Blvd., Exposition Park, 213-763-DINO, www.amnh.org) Open Mon. - Fri. 9:30 a.m. - 5 p.m., Sat. - Sun. 11 a.m. - 5 p.m., $8, $5.50 seniors & students over 12, $2 children ages 5 to 12, children under 5 free. Free admission the first Tuesday of every month.

*NORTON SIMON MUSEUM OF ART (411 W. Colorado Blvd., Pasadena, 626-449-6840, www.nortonsimon.org) Open Wed. - Sun. noon - 6 p.m., Fri. noon - 9 p.m., $8, $4 seniors, children under 18 & students free.

**PACIFIC ASIA MUSEUM (46 N. Los Robles Ave., Pasadena, 626-449-2742pacificasiamuseum.org) Open Wed. - Sun. 10 a.m. - 5 p.m., Fri. 10 a.m. - 8 p.m., $7, $5 seniors & students, children 12 & under free.

**PAGE MUSEUM AT THE LA BREA TAR PITS (5801 Wilshire Blvd., 323-857-6311, www.tarpits.org) Open Sat. and Sun. 10 a.m. - 5 p.m., Mon. - Fri. 9:30 a.m. - 5 p.m., $7, $4.50 students (ages 13 and up) & seniors, $2 children ages 5-12, under 5 free. Free admission the first Tuesday of every month.

**PEPPERDINE UNIVERSITY FREDERICK R. WEISMAN MUSEUM OF ART (24255 Pacific Coast Highway, 310-456-4851, www.pepperdine.edu/arts/museum) Closed Monday, Tues. - Sun. 11 a.m. - 5 p.m., free.

*SANTA MONICA MUSEUM OF ART (Bergamot Station, 2525 Michigan Ave., 310-586-6488, www.smmoa.org) Open Tues. - Sat. 11 a.m. - 6 p.m., $3 suggested donation.

SKIRBALL CULTURAL CENTER (2701 N. Sepulveda Blvd., 310-440-4500, www.skirball.org) Closed Monday, Tues. - Sat. noon - 5 p.m., Sun. 11 a.m. - 5 p.m., $8, $6 students & seniors, children under 12 free. Thursday noon – 9 p.m., free.

*SOUTHWEST MUSEUM (234 Museum Dr., 323-221-2164) Closed Monday, open 10 a.m. - 5 p.m., $7.50, $5 seniors & students, $3 ages 2-12, children under 2 free.

**UCLA FOWLER MUSEUM OF CULTURAL HISTORY (310-825-4361, fowler.ucla.edu) Open Wed. - Sun. noon - 5 p.m., Thurs. noon - 8 p.m., free.

**USC FISHER GALLERY (823 Exposition Blvd., 213-740-4561, www.usc.edu/fishergallery) Open Mon. - Fri. noon - 5 p.m., closed Sat. & Sun., free.

MISS PAMELA'S TOP TEN
A Guide to Groovy Rockin' LA Haunts Past & Present
Pamela des Barres

I am one of those rare birds actually born in the City of Angels. Other than a few months in Manhattan and a year in London, I have resided in this embarrassingly abundant Land of Plenty my entire life. I wish I'd been of age when Dean Martin's knowing puss lit up Dino's restaurant, beaming cheeky neon on the Strip. I also missed out on the Villa Capri, hidden discreetly behind Hollywood Boulevard, but I've studied the shiny black and whites featuring Sammy Davis, Jr. nose to nose with James Dean. The unlikely twosome had been celebrating Frank Sinatra's birthday within those hallowed show biz walls, which is now just a run-down parking lot. Sigh.

Yes, I wish I could have cozied up with the Rebel and certain members of the Rat Pack, but I had my fun a few years later. Narrowing down my fave hangs to a mere ten has been quite a task, especially since I have been encouraged to traverse the decades and include sadly now-defunct specialty spots. I do intend, however, to bring you up-to-date, as I still frequent musical establishments on a regular basis. You can't keep an old flowerchild down, so don't even try.

1. PANDORA'S BOX (no longer standing) Just the name of this long-lost club evokes purple swirling passion, doesn't it? Situated on its very own island on the corner of Sunset and Crescent Heights, this welcoming hippie haven accommodated all manner of musicians, long-haired poets, trippy types, and fading Beats. It was in the middle of a big yard, sweetly encircled by a white picket fence, where we all lounged on the grass, smoking pot, deeply discussing the upcoming revolution. Steven Stills wrote *For What It's Worth* — with those religious lyrics: "Stop, hey, what's that sound/everybody look what's goin' down..." — the night of the infamous front-page Sunset Strip Riots. *They* were going to close down our club to make way for a three-way turn signal, and a spontaneous protest erupted. Even though a couple thousand of us sat cross-legged in the middle of Sunset Boulevard, stopping traffic for miles, the pigs came tromping at us with billy-clubs, and Pandora's Box closed anyway.

2. CIRO'S (8433 Sunset Blvd., West Hollywood) This once sexy showfolk hub is now the **Comedy Store**, situated next door to the rock and roll **Hyatt (Riot) House** (8401 Sunset Blvd., 323-656-1234). There were still fading remnants of old-school glamour when I saw my favorite band, the Byrds, play there in 1965. The same backstage door still faces the street, and all I had to do was knock on that very door, which was opened by Jim (not yet Roger Wilco Over and Out) McGuinn, who kindly handed me a joint and ushered me backstage. Lucky for me... as I was underage and had not yet gotten my fake ID. The word 'Groupie' didn't exist yet, but I was on my way.

3. THE WHISKY A GO-GO (8901 Sunset Blvd., West Hollywood, 310-652-4202, thewhiskyagogo.com) My second home for many years, this absurdly hep, hip, trendsetting nightspot is featured heavily in many of my most scintillating, dreamy memories. I saw Jimi Hendrix set the universe on fire there, I saw Led Zeppelin take over the world, saw The Who blast the walls apart, saw Jim Morrison pull his leather trousers down, saw Gram Parsons weep while singing a George Jones song, saw Janis Joplin on mescaline, and watched lavender and orange paint melt off the club and run down the Sunset Strip gutters. Mick Jagger swept me out of one of the red leather booths and took me home one steamy night; and my all-girl group, The GTO's performed our fist gig, backed by the Mothers of Invention on the Whisky dance floor.

4. THE GALAXY Two doors west from the Whisky was a dark, intimate little club owned by a brassy, bossy broad, Rose Deitch. She wasn't one for letting the hippies in free but my girlfriend, Iva Turner, and I became scantily-clad go-go dancers so we could dribble and drool over the house band, Iron Butterfly. The original lead singer, the late ultra-great Daryl De Loach was the naughtiest, haughtiest, shiniest, horniest rockgod the Sunset Strip had to offer. And I offered my grateful services to him upstairs in the Galaxy broom closet on many occasions.

5. BIDO LIDO'S (once located at 1607 N. Ivar, Hollywood) Hidden away on North Ivar, and down a couple flights of rickety rock stairs, was the mysterious Bido Lito's, a stuffy little dive where Love and the Doors played regularly. I remember running into Sky Saxon of the Seeds on those stairs and listening to his far-out, far-fetched concepts until I couldn't see straight. Later, I sat on the back of a booth, sniffing a rude wah-wah substance called Trimar, when I saw the *real* Jim Morrison for the first time. He teetered dangerously on stage, wailing like he was trapped in his own personal Hades and dead set on pulling us into the flames. I was higher that anyone should ever be, and went straight down Dante's psychedelic inferno with the Lizard King.

6. 303 NORTH LAUREL AVE. This isn't a club or a restaurant, but was once the site of some fascinating Swingin' Sixties goings-on. Vito Paulekas and his wife, Szou, lived and worked here, teaching us wide-eyed teens how to dance, dress, sculpt, completely cut loose and shake off any leftover vestiges of normalcy. Szou had one of the very first vintage clothing stores on the first floor, Vito taught free-form dance and sculpting in the basement, and they lived on the top floor in a crazy cluttered madcap kingdom with their gorgeous blond toddler, Godot. I became part of his troupe of freaks, and we danced wildly at love-ins and with various rock bands, getting in free to all the clubs. Szou and Vito lived here until they were asked un-politely to leave the country after authorities got wind of Vito's penchant for underage nymphs.

7. THE CHEETAH CLUB (no longer standing) Located at the end of the Santa Monica Pier, this cavernous venue once held those wicked '30s dance marathons, where people actually died dancing to win prize money. The Cheetah was short-lived, but divinely memorable. It was here that I ran into Frank Zappa the second time (the first was at the Sunset Strip Riot) and found myself joyously rolling all over the floor with the Grand Poo-Bah Mother of Invention himself. One night Vito colorfully painted a naked Miss Sparky, and had her gyrate and twist on a giant piece of paper he had laid out on the floor, creating a unique piece of art. I have a photo of myself, half naked, arms stretched up to the heavens, dancing on stage with a band I can't quite recall.

8. THE TROUBADOUR (9081 Santa Monica Blvd., West Hollywood, 310-276-6168, www.troubadour.com) More of a folkie joint in the late Sixties, early Seventies, it still had its glorious moments. Once again, I was barely clothed, tossing daisies at an astonished Waylon Jennings' cowboy-booted feet while he tore up the joint. That same night, I was introduced to my absolute hero, Bob Dylan, by Willie Nelson. It doesn't get much better than that, even though Bob's handshake was a tad on the limp side. One of my saddest moments happened at the Troubadour. The last time I saw Gram Parsons, he was trying to reach his drug dealer on the phone in the lobby. He looked forlorn and worn out. His sweet hazel eyes seemed to be saying "I'm so damn sorry," and as I recalled in my book, *I'm With the Band*, his elegant, long-fingered hands hung at his sides like forgotten flowers.

9. THE LOG CABIN (no longer standing) Way back in 1915, Tom Mix, the Hollywood cowboy, built a massive log cabin on the corner of Laurel Canyon Boulevard and Lookout Mountain Drive. Apparently when his beloved horse, Blue, died and went to pony heaven, Tom buried him under the bowling alley in the basement. It was there, in between tossing dented wooden balls down the alley, that the GTO's wrote the

14 songs for our album, *Permanent Damage*. Frank Zappa resided in the cabin at that time, along with his wife Gail and baby, Moon Unit. One of my Vito dancing partners, Miss Christine, was Moon's nanny. She and I spent many exquisitely unforgettable days and nights in front of the humungous rock fireplace, gabbing it up with the encouraging Mr. Z, a genius at just about everything.

10. THE CINEMA BAR (3967 Sepulveda Blvd., Culver City, 310-390-1328, www.myspace.com/thecinemabar) Here we are at the end of the list, and there are dozens more locations I could go on and on about: the Ambassador Hotel, the Palomino, the Hullaballoo Club, the Experience, Rodney's English Disco.... But the time is now and the Cinema Bar is where I spend a lot of my nights these days, still dancing up quite a storm. Long before I walked through the door, I'd been intrigued by the perfectly vintage red neon 'Cinema' sign poking crimson beams through the Culver City fog. It reminded me of platform heels and ruby lips, men with fancy felt hats and sideways glances. I was invited to a birthday bash at the tiny old-fashioned bar a couple of years ago and Mike Stinson was playing his authentic bitchen brand of country music. After his set, I made it clear that I thought we could have some fun together. He still plays the Cinema Bar, we're still having a blast, and occasionally I still go out scantily clad.

UNDERAGE DRINKING
Calm Down, It's Mommy and Daddy's Turn!
Libby Molyneaux

The family that drinks together... wait, that would be wrong. Once you have a kid, cocktail hour is replaced with bath-time, storybooks, and making din-din. But is it unreasonable for parents to want to relax over a libation in a public watering hole with kids in tow? Maybe, maybe not. Please don't send the PC police after us. We're not talking about Lee Remick getting sloshed in front of her toddler daughter in *The Days of Wine and Roses*. The suggested scenario here is to enjoy a cold adult beverage in a spot where your offspring is welcome and can nosh on a snack and sing along with the jukebox. And don't tell us that Chuck E. Cheese serves beer. That's not what we're after. (So does the LA Zoo, but that's not what we're after either.)

Though many bars in LA sound like fun places: the Frolic Room, Cowboy Palace, Liquid Kitty, the Tattle Tale Room — where a toddler could work off energy while Mom and Dad try to restore theirs — you need a place that's not too quiet, has outdoor seating and a relaxed clientele, which pretty much eliminates any place hip. We picked the following bars based not only on comfort, food, and atmosphere criteria, but also on how we would feel if there was a tantrum or spilling incident. Also, we're thinking late weekend afternoon, not last call (*that* would really be wrong).

THE ABBY (692 N. Robertson Blvd., W. Hollywood, 310-289-8410, www.abbeyfoodandbar.com) Kids make a mess with the grilled chicken sticks with peanut sauce. Parents sip a lovely cocktail on the curtained cabana lounger. Kids decide to play hide-and-seek under curtained cabana lounger. Giggling ensues.

CAT & FIDDLE (6530 Sunset Blvd., Hollywood, 323-468-3800) Well-poured black-and-tans and a shady table make for a heavenly pub experience. The littlest ones will love the fountain in the lovely outdoor patio. And just watch their expression when they taste their first malt vinegar. Warning: kids + darts = bad combination. Avoid the food (but not the chips) at all cost.

BIG DEAN'S CAFE (1615 Ocean Front Walk, Santa Monica, 310-393-2666) LA needs more friendly bars like this one, where you're welcome in a wet bathing suit and rollerblades. Beer and wine only. It's just steps from the Santa Monica Pier, so it's perfect for a post-Carousel break. And then it's back on the Carousel again!

RUSTY'S SURF RANCH (256 Santa Monica Pier, 310-393-PIER) Another SM Pier spot, but this one has full bar, outdoor tables and kids' menu, including a root beer float so they can mimic you and your frosty margarita. Evenings, they feature hot local bands (for band info, call 310-393-7346).

BARNEY'S BEANERY (8447 Santa Monica Blvd., W. Hollywood, 323-654-2287) Okay, we don't feel *that* great about ordering a pitcher of Harp and a glass of milk with a straw at this famous rockin' dive, but the kids dig the big-screen TVs and dancing to "Paradise City" and you certainly don't have to worry about them spilling: Janis Joplin vomited on most every surface here in the '50s

RED LION TAVERN (2366 Glendale Blvd., Silver Lake, 323-662-5337). Amaze your child as you down a yard of some weird European brew on the brick patio... but beware of smokers tainting wee ones' immaculate innards.

NEPTUNE'S NET (42505 Pacific Coast Hwy., Malibu on the Ventura County line, 310-457-3095). Sandy feet are the norm here at this PCH biker/surfer hangout. Get a seat on the dirt hill next to the parking lot and feed the birds breadcrumbs while you enjoy a cold beer or wine cooler.

KIDDING AROUND
E.A. Gehman

Holy Crap, Darling Reader, do NOT bring your children to LA. That's right. Leave 'em at home with a two-week supply of Easy Mac and pop-top Dinty Moore, then come and enjoy our hedonistic, self-indulgent Land of Eternal Immaturity all on your own, without impediment of any whining, entitled little brats telling you what to do. Oh wait, wait, wait, those are the studio heads. *Your* children are fetching and well-mannered, and should be shown a good time, here in the land of Inappropriate Billboards and Murderers Who Get Away With Murder. So, if you please, a few humble suggestions, mostly based on nostalgia for an era when children liked to play with sticks and mud and ponies, and weren't able to avidly watch your seatmate's laptop porn on the flight out here.

Griffith Park

Griffith Park is the LA equivalent of Central Park though, at more than 4,200 acres, it's five times as large. There's lots of great stuff to do, including museums, a golf course, hiking trails, and picnic areas. This wonderful place has been the same since I was a child in the Victorian Era, though today the crime rate is much lower; venture into the wilderness and there's only a 50-50 chance you'll get mugged by a gang, so good progress has been made! A few attractions are real standouts:

Ponies and Trains — the nickname the locals have given it — is a huge triple-track riding ring with shaggy Shetland ponies committed to a life of hoofing it with little kids on their backs, run by Mexican caballeros who may well moonlight as rent boys. There are slow, medium and fast ponies, which, as it turns out, are a metaphor for life in general, yes? The ponies are safe clodhoppers who've been toting kids around forever. My little girl began her equestrian career here, on the slows, and now has ruined my life by becoming a nationally-ranked hunter who needs to be chaperoned at events all over the country, and which has led to the demolition of both my career and my psyche — but I digress. You probably won't be that lucky, but it's still worth a little recreational visit. In the same fun compound is a toy-size train that will cruise your whole family around a half-acre of billion-dollar real estate, complete with a conductor and a gas-powered engine that'll make you ill if you sit in one of the front cars. Run for the caboose! Along the train tracks are surreal little still-lives worthy of Damian Hearst; peeling-painted Bambies and Elves with Mushrooms, a miniature Ghost Town... the pony rides are about a buck a head and the train ride is the same. DO visit; Pretty soon, like everything else innocent and fun here in Hell A, this will be turned to dust when Griffith Park is "renovated" (that's our fancy, post-modern term for *demolished by assholes with no souls...* er, I mean the Planning Commission).

Across the street from Ponies 'n Trains is the one and only monument to the architect of all our fates in this profound behemoth of a Metropolis, William Mulholland, the man who stole water from the North so that we here in the South might party on. It's a lovely fountain that's rainbow-lit at night; you can indulge your historical yayas; the kids can ditch all your loose change. Watch *Chinatown* later that night in your hotel room with take-out from the fabulous contempochinese restaurant **Kung Pao Kitty** (6445 Hollywood Blvd., Hollywood, 323-465 0110) while the kids occupy themselves with trinkets from **Traveltown** (5200 Zoo Drive, 323-662-5824) which is just up the road in Griffith Park from Ponies 'n' Trains. TT is yet another homage to the horseless carriage in Griffith Park; only in addition to another fun toy-size train for the family to ride, it has an amazing collection of real train cars from all eras, which you can climb all over and examine up close. The indoor transportation museum is wonderful, and it has one of the most complex, absurdly small-scale, model trains in the country behind a massive Plexiglas viewing wall (I think it's double O scale—short for the Ongoing Orgasm it gives model train enthusiasts). Your kids will be fascinated with the tiny trains — passenger and freight — and with the microscopic scenarios of glorified middle-American mid-century life. YOU will be fascinated with the hipster nerd dudes who make this their life's work, and who are such a combination of hot and post-modern dork, it'll keep you pondering the existential nature of *passion* for days after. Fanfuckingtastic. And free except for the train-ride tix!

Double back and you'll run smack into the **Griffith Park Carousel** (4730 Crystal Springs Dr., 323-913-4688, www.lacity.org/RAP/dos/parks/facility/griffithPk.html) an absolutely amazing late 1800s restored carousel with beautiful hand-painted scenes, and unbelievably haunting and beautiful creatures and chariots for you to ride on. A wondrous restored pipe organ, and an amazingly swift circuit, so eat lunch *after* or you'll be seeing your meal for the second time... Ages: Adult if playful, nostalgic, and/or baked; kids infant-12 (if not jaded by pop culture and addicted to IMing) Otherwise, 10. (And if your 10-year-old is beyond this, you're almost beyond help and should be marched to the provinces and re-educated.)

Bob's Big Boy, Burbank

Did Bob have an obsession with his best part, or was he just unaware of terminology that has existed since, oh, Roman times? At any rate, he created a chain of wonderful burger joints with yummy better-than-diner food, and the restaurant in Burbank (4211 Riverside Dr., 818-843-9334, www.bobs.net) is also a perfectly restored architectural landmark, designated a State Point of Historical Interest in 1993. It hosts a rockingly fun vintage car show every Friday night between 6 and 10 p.m. in the parking lot, presented by **The Road Kings** (www.roadkingsburbank.com). The restaurant also has "Back to the '50s" carhop service on Saturday and Sunday nights, between 6 and 10 p.m. Great cars, great people watching, yum food if you're not a vegan paranoid. All the burgers rock, and they're known for the chili spaghetti and the ice cream sundaes. Free helium balloons after din-din. And before the nighttime fun, see if you can take in a show at the **Falcon Theatre** (4252 W. Riverside Dr., 818-955-8101) across the street. Owned and run by tv jillionaire Gerry Marshall, their fare is frequently kid-friendly and awesome.

The Artful Dodgers

If you're in town any time during baseball season, go to a Dodgers Game. **Dodger Stadium** (1000 Elysian Park Ave., LA, www.dodgers.mlb.com) is one of the jewels in the crown of major league baseball, an enormous old-school ballpark. To really make your trip meaningful, be sure to tell your kids the history of the Stadium, how the long-time community of farm workers who lived in Chavez Ravine was demolished, ruining the lives of multiple generations to build the ballpark and bring a shinin' bit of the sports/industrial complex to our sad little confluence of citrus trees and defense contracting. Find a kid-friendly yet still harrowing description of the tragedy at **Chavez Ravine** (www.toonist.com/flash/ravine.html)

Adios, Pajaros

There are a lot of birds in this town. Please go visit them. Birds at the beach: Bring bread, the gulls'll come to you: **Santa Monica Beaches** (www.santa-monica-beach.com), lifeguard stations 19-24, strung like a string of pretty pearls on either side of the Pier. **The Swans at Hotel Bel Air** (from Los Angeles, take Sunset heading west, go right up Stone Canyon Road. Stop at the Pink Behemoth. 310-472-1211, www.hotelbelair.com) Swans live in the creek that runs through the property, and are all ethereal and fab in black as well as white. They're also mean, so don't offer them any food, just look from the bridge. Act as if you're staying at the Hotel, and you can wander the acres of beautifully planted grounds amidst the pink bungalows. Go on a Sunday and you can crash someone's multi-million-dollar wedding. **Birds at Tree People** (12601 Mulholland Drive, Beverly Hills, 818-753-4600, www.TreePeople.org) is located in a lovely, preserved bit of the Santa Monica Mountain chain, which has dedicated itself to being a conservator of the "urban forest." Great hiking trails, a visitor center, great view of birds: Indigenous wrens and warblers, lots of red-tailed hawks inscribing lazy letters in the sky above; big-ass hooty owls, and the occasional awe-inspiring Golden Eagle. **Birds at the Los Angeles Zoo** (5333 Zoo Dr., LA, 323-644-6400, www.lazoo.org)... you're cheating a bit, but okay, The LA Zoo has lots of bird exhibits; smack-dab after the entrance are all the flamingos, just in case you're keeping up the pink theme from your visit to the Hotel Bel Air. **The Guy with the Parrots on Venice Beach**: **Venice Beach Boardwalk** (www.westland.net/beachcam) Stroll the boardwalk and you'll more than likely run into him. His birds talk, sing, dance, and generally behave in ways outside of nature. Fun! **Birds the Restaurant** (5925 Franklin Ave., LA) You're a cannibal, and want to experience birds a different way, fine: The most amazing chicken wraps, breasts, wings, and onion rings in town. Located in Hollywood, right across from the **Scientology Celebrity Center** (www.theta.com) so you can catch sight of the very special loony birds there, too.

The Museum of Jurassic Technology (9341 Venice Blvd., Culver City, 310-836-6131, www.mjt.org) will screw your mind up as much as your child's, with its fake exhibits presented as realistically as possible, and its incredibly sincere representations of false phenomenon. The geniuses who have art-directed this wondrous place claim that everything's real, and that they are basing themselves on the long tradition of European private court museums and curiosity cabinets, which were the sole province of the royal and anointed. Whatever. This joint is unbelievably awesome, and confounds even the most jaded-from-exposure-to-too-many-special-effects-in-inappropriate-media child. Sally forth, and be humbled and amazed. And while you're over there in Culver City being amazed, wander across the street and you'll see the façade of **Tara**, from *Gone With the Wind*, which has been turned into an office building for Sony Pictures. The kids will care more about the fact that animated crap is produced here, but you'll weep at the thought that Vivian Leigh and Clark Gable once kissed where you are standing now. Also in the same block is the hotel where all the **Munchkins** lived (9400 Culver Blvd.) during the shooting of *The Wizard of Oz*, which was produced on the very same lot. Some pix of a Munchkin reunion at the hotel: (www.beyondtherainbow2oz.com/culverhotel.html)

A *Gone with the Wind* **site** by someone who clearly is a stalker or has some serious Southern-style OCD: (www.sunset angel.com) Jeepers!

Sony Picture Studios, where you can actually take a tour! (323-520-TOUR, www.sonypicturesstudios.com)

Kids Love Gory Things...

... and death, and ghosts, because they've been made baroque and morbid by the media's obsession with violent stories and blood-soaked imagery. Indulge their sensibilities at **Hollywood Forever** (6000 Santa Monica Blvd., Hollywood, CA, 323-469-1181, www.hollywoodforever.com), the most beautiful cemetery in the Wild West, which was historically conserved, preserved and amped up by the only man one of your illustrious Editors and I have ever *both* had a crush on. For the past two decades. Swooningly and relentlessly and hopelessly. Words fail us repeatedly. Our knees grow weak. (Editors' note: SHUUUUUUUT UP! He shall remain nameless, and if he reads this, he'll probably never talk to either one of us...) Oh, wait, wait — we were talking about the cemetery! There are lots of movie stars (or "Hollywood Immortals," as the cemetery management prefers to call them) buried here, as well as other illustrious people, and regular Joes. The grounds are beautiful and well-planted, the mausoleums both impressive and ominous, the monuments sad and thrilling. The Funeral Chapel is wired for worldwide webcasts of services and the "LifeStory" video memorials have the production values of feature films. Bring a blanket and a picnic, a camera and a hanky.

California Cactus Center

The **California Cactus Center** (216 South Rosemead Blvd, Pasadena, 626-795-2788, cactuscenter.com, open 7 days 10 a.m. - 4:30 p.m.) has the most amazing collection of cacti anywhere, and if you lose your balance or mis-step, you'll get a prong stake where no prong belongs. You'll have your appendix removed for free, or your buttcheeks pierced. No, but seriously, cacti have spines in order to increase their surface area to garner moisture, not because they have hostility issues. In the desert, frequently 'mist' or fog is the only water source a cactus plant has, and the prickly spikes help grab these out of the air. Who cares? These cacti looks like amazing alien creatures who were visiting from outer space and accidentally got mummified. Bring toy guns and you can dodge around among the plants and pretend you're in *The Searchers*. You be John Wayne, the kids can be the Injuns he's trying to cleanse from the face of the earth. The place is actually a store, but fancies itself cacti conservators, and welcomes guests to view the collection.

John Wayne tribute page by an obsessive fan (www.jwayne.com). You can see Jaydubs's footprints at **Grauman's**.

Scarier than the Rides at Universal Studios... and Cheaper, Too!

If your kids are thrill junkies and love adrenaline-disorder-inducing things like rollercoaster rides, explain to them that LA is striated with some of the most active earthquake faultlines on the planet, snaking between geological plates that are so unstable they frequently shake like killer Jell-o. Then take the little ones for a ride underground on the **LA Metro** (www.metro.net) which, at a million bucks per foot, is the most expensive subway system in the universe, and could well be entirely amazing in terms of shake and sway the next time a big temblor rocks and rolls us. You'll need a grande supply of Ativan for the hair-raising ride, but the kids will want to tempt fate again and again! Also, local legend has it that the rail line to Downtown smashes through an abandoned graveyard of Chinese railway workers, so you might even have some spectral sightings that are better than **Disneyland**'s Haunted Mansion. To get the most out of your experiment — I mean your experience — check out the **United States Geological Survey website** (www.quake.wr.usgs.gov) for Fun Facts & informative and terrifying pix before you go underground!

When you get to the metro station located at **Hollywood & Highland Mall** (hollywood andhighland.com), restaurants, shops, etc. at — you guessed it — the corner of Hollywood Blvd. and Highland Ave.), pop above ground for a different kind of horror show. H & H is the most ill-conceived and badly designed "mall" in America, with its low-rent shops and sad attempts at packaging and spewing Hollywood history. It has consumed and subsumed **Grauman's Chinese Theatre** (manntheatres.com), the site of many huge premiers, past and present. The courtyard is filled with hand & footprints of real movie stars (as opposed to fake ones like Lindsey) but the main thing you & the kids will be interested in is all the meth addicts dressed up as characters who run the gamut of pop culture from Elmo to Marilyn Monroe to Darth Vader. For a "donated" fee, they'll let you take pix with them! But the real excitement comes when the temperature rises and the crowds thin, and the characters start competing with each other for your attention. Then the entire scene turns into a bad Wim Wenders movie about Mexican Wrestling, and you'll thrill to the sight of Spiderman kicking Chewbacca's ass, or Wonder Woman having a throw-down with Betty Boop. Other than the swearing, it's good old-fashioned fun!

Right upstairs at H & H is the **Kodak Theatre** (6801 Hollywood Boulevard, Hollywood, 323-308-6300, box office hours Mon. - Sat. 10 a.m. - 6 p.m., Sun 10 a.m. - 2:30 p.m., www.kodaktheatre.com) and if you don't feel like dropping coin for whatever cheesy show they have playing (to whit, *Riverdance* seems to be in continuous rotation), you can still admire the portal through which passes the entire cast of the Academy Awards, and *American Idol*. It all happens right here, baby!

If you have more time to explore terrifying earth science, you can take the kids to actually *see* the San Andreas Fault as it rips across the land. About three hours north of Los Angeles is the **Carrizo Plain** (www.santalucia.sierraclub.org/carrizo.html) , where you can walk on the San Andreas Fault as it pops out of the ground. Wowee!!

ART-I-FACTS
Al Ridenour

Back when LA was angry, sporting a Mohawk and playing in a band using an electric grinder to throw sparks at the audience, back when industrial music was actually performed in industrial spaces and wasn't just a nostalgic theme night at a dance club in Encino, the greasy loading docks and flyer-plastered dumpsters of downtown LA were the backdrop for all that was cool. Downtown was the shit! That's what we thought (we hadn't even heard of the Skybar, bless our little hearts).

DOWNTOWN

Downtown is still cool, and is still the thudding heart of an underground arts scene. It's just not that angry anymore. And it happened like this: Everyone knows semi-abandoned stretches of industrial space attract artists. And artists attract people who wish they were artists, and so on down the cultural food chain. At some point around the turn of the century, city redevelopment agencies realized this could be exploited, that it's much safer to have Downtown's alleys crawling with art-happy kids on Ecstasy than indigenous crack addicts hunting for car stereos. LA's no-man's lands were slowly reclaimed by a new arts scene heavily influenced by the more tractable why-can't-we-all-just-get-along optimism of the rave scene.

The hands-down biggest player Downtown, and most influential force in LA's underground arts scene, right now is **Cannibal Flower** (various locations — cannibalflower.com). Since 2000, this jubilantly inclusive experiment in community building and why-can't-we-all-just-be-artists curatorial policy has been responsible for immensely popular electronica-driven "art parties," in an ever-changing variety of spaces, including the dank cloisters of St. Vibiana's Cathedral, the rooftops of taxi-dance halls, and the vaults of the old Crocker Bank Building. Held monthly, Cannibal Flower's massive fifty-plus piece group shows are complemented by solo shows occasionally including underground luminaries like Mark Mothersbaugh, Anthony Ausgang, or Liz McGrath. Equally if not more important to Cannibal Flower's synergistic success are the armies of DJs awaiting their stint on the tables, the live painting displays, fashion shows, performance art, video installations, sword-swallowing, fire-breathing, belly-dancing, fetish-friendly alterna-circus environment.

Frequent site of roving curatorial endeavors such as Cannibal Flower, **Hangar 1018** (1018 S. Santa Fe Ave., 213-239-0602, www.hangar1018.com) also holds "The Max," their in-house third Saturday of the month version of the downtown art party, often featuring as many as thirty painters sloshing paint onto canvases accompanied by music from the studio's stage. Around the corner is the less clubby and more clubhouse-like **Treehouse Gallery** (2345 E. Olympic Blvd., 213-673-

4727, www.thgallery.com), an intimate combination studio, living, and exhibition space, which also holds the occasional poetry slam, and street-side rollerblading competition.

A few blocks north, **Transport Gallery** (1308 Factory Place, 213-623-4099, www.transportgallery.com) has earned its underground cred with an *Adbusters* style show of corporate logo parodies, which the LAPD is said to have busted in April 2005 due to the "aggressive and offensive" nature of the show. Thank god for a little conflict!

To the west, on or between Main and Spring from 2nd to 9th, lies what's enthusiastically been termed **Gallery Row**. Civic boosterism notwithstanding, there's still a bit of underground action in that mixed bag best checked out during the monthly (2nd Thursday) **Downtown Art Walks** (www.downtownartwalk.com). Walks are free and self-guided, and there's also an Art Ride for all you bike culture types.

If your tastes run toward spray-paint, you'll dig Gallery Row's newest inductee, **Crewest: Gallery + Shop** (110 Winston St., 213-627-8272, www.crewest.com) offering hoodies and hip-hop videos alongside large-scale graffiti panels and darling... er... "dope" miniature pre-tagged subway cars. Slightly more diverse is **The Hive Gallery & Studios** (729 S. Spring St., 213-955-9051) who is also Hangar 1018's "The Max" curator. The Hive features first Saturday of the month group shows, a blacklight lounge, video projections, performance painting, live and spun music.

The previously roving **Create: Fixate** (createfixate.com) has more or less found permanent digs in the mezzanine of the **Spring Arts Tower** aka Crocker Bank (453 S. Spring Street). Expanding a bit on Cannibal Flower's hybridization of rave-meets-group-show, Create: Fixate is exploring non-profit status, corporate sponsorship, artists workshops on topics like copyright law, and even pulling in grown-up DJs from

KCRW. And if you just can't get enough fire-dancing, stilt-walking, hookah-smoking, el-wire-wearing manufactured decadence, you should also check with the **Do Lab** (www.thedolab.com), producers of events like the unassumingly named "Lucent L' Amour: A Visionary Love Fest" at St. Vibiana's Cathedral.

Across the street from St. Vib's, is the refreshingly grungy underground stalwart, **The Smell** (247 S. Main, 213-625-4325, www.thesmell.org) where far-side-of-indie bands find themselves booked alongside analog noisemakers, streetwise modern dance, punky sideshow acts, and the occasional video or sound installation.

Chinatown also has its smattering of underground spaces with **Betalevel** (963 N. Hill Street, down the alley, look for the red door, www.Betalevel.com) most literally fitting that definition with its speakeasy-style basement setting. A friendly DIY feel pervades gatherings held here, which include performances, classes, screenings, lectures, dances, readings, tournaments, and digital music swaps. Promising more in the same vein, **Fringe Exhibitions** (504 Chung King Court, 213-613-0160, www.fringexhibitions.com) opened recently amid the apocalyptic fanfare of a Survival Research Labs show, the never-quite-legal and quintessentially underground art world's answer to the demolition derby. Specializing in electronic media art, **Telic Arts Exchange** (975 Chung King Rd., 213-344–6137, www.telic.info.com) may be a little highbrow to get your underground juices flowing, but they have played host to some fascinating work like Natalie Jeremijenkjo's 2004 installation in which visitors piloted aquatic robotic geese to interact with squawkingly real specimens.

Another hotspot away from central Downtown is the **Brewery Art Colony** (600 Moulton Ave.), best visited during the semi-annual **Brewery Artwalks** (www.brewery

artwalk.com) when a little mingling will open the doors to underground parties where they haul out the Tesla Coils, flame-throwers, and giant glowing flowers you thought only existed at Burning Man. Two spaces of note there: **Abundant Sugar** (618A Moulton Ave., www.abundantsugar.com), a studio/performance space offering workshops in dance, yoga, trapeze, and midwifery; and also **Swift Gallery**, (676 S Avenue 21 St. 200, 213-403-0166, www.swiftgallery.org), an artist-run exhibition/performance space for "provocative art and culture," as embodied in a recent showing of artist Bob Partington's Briefcase Tagging Device and Spray Paint Cannon.

Over on the other side of downtown near USC is the **Velaslavasay Panorama** (1122 West 24th St., 213-746-2166, www.panoramaonview.org). Located in the deco-era **Union Theater**, it's ostensibly an exhibition hall for the 19th-century novelty genre of the 360-degree landscape painting. Underground by virtue of its sheer eccentricity, the Panorama supplements the occasional lag in interest in 19th century panorama painting with interesting theatrical/performance offerings reflecting proprietor Sara Velas' Cal Arts roots.

And speaking of Cal Arts, it would be remiss to ignore **REDCAT, the Roy and Edna Disney/CalArts Theater** (631 West 2nd St., 213-237-2800, www.redcat.org) which, despite the "D word," has been known to present delightfully transgressive works like Ron Athey and Juliana Snapper's ecstatically full-frontal torture-fest, *Judas Cradle*, and others that would have Walt spinning in his grave.

THE EASTSIDE

The Eastside makes a nod to the Cannibal-Flower-style "art party" with clubby happenings at the **Hear Gallery & Studios** (2206 Beverly Blvd., www.theheargallery.com). But the most significant contribution to the underground scene is certainly the venerable **La Luz de Jesus** (4633 Hollywood Blvd., 323-666-7667, www.laluzdejesus.com) happily tucked into the boutique-cum-bookstore-cum-alternative-retail-reality of **Wacko**. Dubbed "the Peggy Guggenheim of Lowbrow," La Luz curator Billy Shire has, since 1986, serves art-hungry hipsters all manner of outsider art, pop surrealism, hot-rod fantasies, Catholic trauma, and cheesecake, introducing underground superstars like Robert Williams, Manuel Ocampo, and Joe Coleman to a wider public. La Luz also organizes the **Eastside Art Crawl** (www.laluzdejesus.com/artcrawl/artcrawl.htm), usually falling on the third weekend in September.

Just a block or so away is **Rosemary's Billygoat Odditorium** (4519 Sunset Blvd., 323-666-GOAT, www.rosemarysbillygoat.com/odditorium).Brought to you by everyone's favorite Satan-lovin' heavy metal costume-rock parody, Rosemary's Billygoat, the Odditorium's in-store gallery shows a variety of art made by artists who will probably spend all eternity in hell. First Friday of the month openings are enlivened by eccentric stage performances and beer served from an ice-filled coffin. Also a good time to check out the boutique's regular inventory of unholy novelties, toys, clothes and accessories stitched together from dead things.

Further down Sunset, deep into the mercilessly hip center of Silver Lake, you'll find the similarly inclined **Sometimes Madness is Wisdom Gallery and Shoppe** (3208 West Sunset Blvd., 323-660-5020, sometimesmadnessiswisdom.com). A bit less hellfire camp, a bit more Victoriana and silk, this elegant cabinet of curiosities features a small gallery, primarily for photography of a dark and pervy nature. Next door is **Gallery Revisited** (3204 Sunset Blvd., 626-253-5266, www.galleryrevisted.com), a transplant from the downtown art world showing photography, paintings, sculpture, and mixed media ("mixed" including "Gummi Bears, Felt, Punk-Rock, Paper, Plastic, Cleaning Supplies, Oils, Thread, Lights, Sculpy, Vinyl, Wood.") Shows addressing issues like consumerism speak to both critical and casual art lovers, and some pieces can be had for less than $50. Nearby, you'll find **Junc Gallery** (4017 Sunset Blvd., 626-298-3014, www.juncgallery.com), a slick but youthful gallery boasting some witty shows including an early installation of a thousand-plus drawings executed on Post-its. Kittycorner from there: **Maker** (4008 Santa Monica Blvd., 323-662-2524) an alternative studio/exhibition space with quarterly shows that have sometimes involved Butoh or performance sculpting staged on a flatbed parked in front of the gallery.

Should you feel truly inspired by the sheer artiness of the neighborhood, you might want to hook up with Craft Captain, Julianna (JP) Parr. Every Wednesday night (9 p.m. - midnight) she hosts **Craft Night** behind the jukeboxes at **Akbar** (4356 Sunset Blvd., www.crafthead.com), a gluey, sparkly, cocktail-enlivened evening. If you're looking for another kind of inspiration, and you need practice drawing really butch musculature, don't forget that the **Tom of Finland Foundation** (1421 Laveta Terrace, 213-250-1685, www.tomof finlandfoundation.org) has monthly life drawing workshops. While there, you may be able to check out the by-appointment-only collections of everyone's favorite leather-daddy fantasy artist.

Free workshops are offered by the **Echo Park Film Center** (1200 N. Alvarado St., 213-484-8846, www.echo parkfilmcenter.org), a micro-cinema with a social conscience, hosting Thursday night film screenings of ultra-indie documentaries, experimental films, and films made by participants in the Center's programs (i.e., neighbor kids). Next door is **Machine Project** (1200 D North Alvarado St., 213-

483-8761, www.machineproject.com) a sublimely alternative art space presenting mainly interactive experiences, poetically framed by curator Mark Allen. Past events have included a chemist's lecture on why wrinkle-free pants stay that way; a room-size working model of an erupting volcano; an exhibition of mathematically crocheted models of hyperbolic space; a live battle between several dozen armored knights, and the chance to undergo the experience of being buried alive. Many events are free, but please hand them wads of cash because LA doesn't let stuff like this live long.

Two more noteworthies along Glendale Boulevard: **Ghetto Gloss Gallery** (2380 Glendale Blvd., 323-912-0008, www.ghettogloss.com) in Silver Lake is another joint for edgy, hipster-friendly art (monthly openings are sometimes rocked by live indie bands). They're also working other angles, running an artists' boutique, publishing in-house art books, even renting outsider art for films and television. A bit further down Glendale in Atwater Village, you'll find **Black Maria Gallery** (3137 Glendale Blvd, 323-660-9393, www.black mariagallery.com) a relative newcomer showing fresh, provocative work often with a social or political subtext.

There's an interesting pocket of theaters and boutiques around Melrose and Heliotrope in East Hollywood. Tucked behind LA's premiere underground video store **Mondo Video A-Go-Go** is **Il Corral** (662 N. Heliotrope Dr., 323-663-0137, www.ilcorral.net), a grittily intimate house party of a venue that operates under the motto "noise is the new punk rock." Along with noisy amplitude modulations, there's the occasional blood-vomiting performance artist, experimental puppet show, and other risk-taking performances. Around the corner is **Clair Obscur Gallery** (4310 Melrose Ave, 323-662-6693 www.clairobscurgallery.com) where the art seems rather darkly preoccupied, with offerings like a solo show by Manson family alumnus Bobby Beausoleil and fetishy photographic studies.

HOLLYWOOD (North & West Hollywood too)

A bit further along into Hollywood proper, there's a few more venues where the art takes a grotesque turn. As you may surmise from the euphonious name, **Dapper Cadaver** (5519 Hollywood Blvd., 323-962-1924, www.dappercadaver.com) is in fact a Goth-ware boutique, but along with the clothes, pickled things, and household accessories made with bones, Cadaver features monthly rotations of visual art as well as cabaret, puppets, and other eccentric performances staged in its intimate sit-down theater space. **Gunn & Co.'s Empire Amusement Hall** (6470 Santa Monica Blvd., 323-270-2518, www.empireamusementhall.com) is an actual theater on Santa Monica Boulevard's Theater Row; but it's a theater you would visit if you are in the mood to see someone drive a nail up his nose — or anything involving a bed of nails. Along with the sideshow stunts, the space hosts an interesting array of burlesque, magic, one-acts, and independent films. Between performances, check out the lobby's collection of headhunters' trophies, voodoo dolls, and stuffed baby elephant, allegedly tracing its lineage to P.T. Barnum's very own collection. (Editors' note: Will somebody *please* buy us one of the pickled cobras housed in a Thai booze bottle that they carry in the lobby?)

And while we're talking dark, up in North Hollywood, there's **California Institute of Abnormal Arts/CIA** (11334 Burbank Blvd., North Hollywood, 818-506-6353, www.ciab normalarts.com), a venue that tends to host art-damage bands, vaudeville, and more indescribable things involving Theremins, stripping midgets, and the like. Much more than a performance space, it's also been called a mini-Smithsonian of sideshow ephemera. Often as entertaining as whatever's on stage, the awe-inspiring collection scattered throughout the warren of rooms, halls, and patio includes a dead fairy, the severed arm of a French nobleman, the alleged head of Bigfoot, and more.

On a more serious note, there is **LACE/Los Angeles Contemporary Exhibitios** (6522 Hollywood Blvd, 323-957-1777, www.artleak.org). Now more than a quarter of a century old, LACE was early supporter of underground artists like Mike Kelley and Karen Finley, and though perhaps not quite as incandescent as it was during its '80s-'90s Downtown incarnation, it still carries on with provocative (and often free) programming. Events run the gamut from a neighborhood walk led by maturing bad-boy artist Paul McCarthy to performances by youngsters like Dude Dogg, "visual artists that wear dog costumes as they perform rock'n'roll covers in a style that is excitingly sloppy, exuberant, raw, and energetic."

In the consumer-frenzied area between La Brea and Fairfax, there's a handful of galleries where the market potential of underground art gets a workout. **Merry Karnowsky Gallery** (170 South La Brea Ave., 323-933-4408, www.mkgallery.com) may not feel particularly edgy set amid those chi-chi antique shops, but it does represent some underground heavyweights like Todd Schorr, Becca, and Shepard Fairey. In a more youthful setting, **Gallery Nineteen Eighty Eight** (7020 Melrose Ave., 323-937-7088, www.nineteeneightyeight.com) shows rising stars like Luke Chueh, Joe Ledbetter, Thomas Han and Greg "Crayola" Simkins. Down near the corner of La Brea on Venice is the equally youthful **project:** (5016 Venice Blvd. 323-283-1733, www.project.biz) showing fresh and often funny street-savvy work. And the tendrils of Cannibal Flower have taken root in with **thinkspace** (675 Spaulding Ave., 323-653-2520, www.thinkspacegallery.com) which is a more-or-less traditionally operating gallery undertaken as collaborative venture with **Sour Harvest** (www.sourharvest.com), an outstanding website for tracking the LA art events of a hip and hipper flavor.

In West Hollywood , **New Image Art Gallery** (7908 Santa Monica Blvd., 323-654-2192, www.newimageartgallery.com) has fun, irreverent shows of street and outsider art like a recent installation by Spazmat, the guy responsible for those charming skull-on-a-cellphone graphics pasted up on overpasses and light poles. Besides, your close personal friends Thurston Moore and Kim Gordon have been sighted at openings here.

CULVER CITY & WEST LA

So much to unlearn here. For more than a decade (or at least ever since the *LA Times* squealed "Silver Lake is on fire!"), smirking hipsters have been slinking further South and East in pursuit of ever-cheap rent and ever-greater trendsetter status. For those pilgrims to the East, the notion of a burgeoning art scene flowering on the Westside, in the mythical sunset land of Culver City, is not only improbable but downright insulting. It is, however, what's going on. While Culver City makes no claims to being rock-and-roll, or even underground, it's become pretty damn arty. Even the Trader Joe's in the neighborhood is rumored to have a 12-month waiting list for artists cueing to hang their work over the coffee beans and organic pet food.

As if to squelch any doubt about this, iconic Eastsider Billy Shire of La Luz de Jesus has recently established **Billy Shire Fine Arts** (5790 Washington Blvd., 323-297-0600, www.billyshirefinearts.com) right across the street from another easterly transplant: **sixspace** (5803 Washington Blvd., 323-932-6200, www.sixspace.com). A refugee from

Downtown, sixspace is a smart, fun gallery that seems to have drawn energy from the Downtown "art party" scene without losing sight of more rigorous approaches to art. This synthesis is nicely reflected in curator Caryn Coleman's daily high and low of the LA scene in http://art.blogging.la/.

Down the street **BLK/MKT Gallery** (6009 Washington Blvd., 310-837-1989, www.blkmrktgallery.com) shows lots of work inspired by zine and comic artists, with occasional forays further afield, such as a recent group show of plush animals or Peter Beste's photographic survey of Norwegian Black Metal. The **Lab101 Gallery** (8530-B Washington Blvd., 310-558-0911, www.thelab101.com) shows a similar mix with perhaps a bit more emphasis on street and skater culture, and occasional deviations like a 2005 show of artist-altered recycling cans. The Lab101 occasionally treads into more commercial territory with deep-pocket image-building support from Puma, Freshjive Clothing, and Scion. Scion even runs its own gallery in the Culver City arts nest, showing exactly the same kinds of work by exactly the same kinds of artists — thereby giving us all plenty of fodder for our now-tired comments about the rapid commodification of underground culture.

A significantly more DIY space somewhat outside the Culver City hotbed is **Basswerks** (5411 W. Adams, 323-939-253, www.basswerks.net), a studio exhibition space with playfully-themed shows and laidback atmosphere, emphasis on VJ performances, and the occasional BBQ.

At a stately remove from world of Scion, spray-paint, or anything involving glow sticks, stands one of LA's greatest art treasures: **The Museum of Jurassic Technology** (9341 Venice Blvd., 310-836-6131, www.mjt.org). In part a sly parody on museum institutionalism, in part poetic meditation, it's dark warren of studiously mounted displays clarifying the nature of the stink ants of Camaroon, Noah's Ark, and bats that fly through solid matter, has slowly been augmented by a series of new and rotating exhibits including eerily twinkling nocturnal trailer park dioramas, a look at eccentric Jesuit polymath Athanasius Kircher, and most recently an upstairs tea room and theater offering hourly screenings of the films, *Levsha, the Cross-Eyed Lefty from Tula* and *The Steel Flea*.

Next door is the equally esoteric **Center for Land Use Interpretation** (9331 Venice Blvd., 310-839-5722, clui.org) responsible for lyrically framed exhibits, presentations, and field trips exploring our relationship to regions beyond those traversed during normal urban life — anything from lectures by a septuagenarian postcard-maker to bus trips to airplane graveyards. Though the tours are not exactly cheap, CLUI's impressive online database of curious landmarks may also inspire you to strike out on your own.

An institution of a different sort — and another that predates the Westside art boom — is West LA's **Giant Robot Store** (2015 Sawtelle Blvd, 310-478-1819, giantrobot.com) now operating a gallery across the street: **GR2** (2026 Sawtelle Blvd., 310-445-9276). Started in 1994 as a humble zine exploring the sometimes-bizarre collisions of Asian and American pop culture, the zine went glossy, developed a cult following, and eventually expanded its empire with a store specializing in Asian toys, graphic novels, T-shirts, and the like. The art shown by GRS is of course related, occasionally riffing on traditional Asian forms, but more likely to explore Asian-American minglings. There's also a recently opened Silver Lake store next to **June**, called **Gallery: GSL** (4017 Sunset Blvd., 323-662-GRLA).

SANTA MONICA

Surely the least "underground" of any of the areas mentioned, Santa Monica still trumps, well... Encino. First, there is **Highways Performance Space** (1651 18th St., 310-315-1459, highwaysperformance.org), the former headquarters of that most remarkable beast: *High Performance*, a nationally circulated magazine strictly devoted to an art form everyone loves to hate. Like LACE, Highways may not be quite as excitingly combative as when Jesse Helms was flailing at the NEA, but this may just represent and overall climatic change. In any case, they still present challenging performances especially focused on concerns of the gay community. Special events and fundraiser parties can also bring in a wilder crowd. The theater's lobby usually features visual art, as well.

The massive **Bergamot Station Arts Center** (2525 Michigan Ave., Santa Monica) is kind of like the Death Star of the LA art world, but its bigness does not in all cases equal badness. Amid the more desiccated conceptual stuff and the bland garnish for Westside living rooms are a couple underground-style gems. **Copro Nason Gallery** (unit T-5, 310-829-2156, www.copronason.com) is a fairly new transplant slowly expanding from its first love of 1960s hotrod/beatnik/cocktail culture into other rough-and-tumble forms, including a memorable show of works by freak-rockers Daniel Johnston and Mark Mothersbaugh.

The politically dissident **Track 16** (Unit C-1, 310-264-4678, www.track16.com) shows established underground types like Raymond Pettibone and Manuel Ocampa and is the fine art rep for tattoo legend Don Ed Hardy. Some of their crowd-drawing shows have included "The Greatest Album Covers That Never Were" and the 2002 "Elective Affinities" installation by David Byrne. Their evening performance series has featured talks by poster artist Robbie Conal, the Nihilist

Film Festival, and music from the very "special" Kids of Widney High. Next door, **Robert Berman Gallery** (units D5/C2, 310-315-1937, www.robertbermangallery.com) can be a bit more highbrow but also shows underground faves like Agit-Pop artist Ron English and the multi-faceted Bill Barminksi.

OUT THERE

It's really been hard to know what constitutes underground art since 1992 when LACMA's "Helter Skelter" show presented the mechanized tree-fucking of Paul McCarthy's "Garden," and now with Toyota going all gangsta at its Scion Space, hosting "revolutionary" graffiti art shows with "revolutionary" titles like "Junta"... well, it's enough to numb the brain. But there was a time before outside was in, and people who marched to the beat of their own aesthetic drum, turning their backyards into junk-pile assemblages, were just plain-simple crazy. A few traces of that world remain in various folk art environments slowly disintegrating around the LA area.

Of course there's the lovely Gaudiesque pottery-crusted spires of **Simon Rodia's Watts Towers** (847-4646 E 107th St, Watts, 213-847-4646), still worth a trip even though hardly visible in their prison-yard setting of scaffolding and razor wire.

Much less famous, and more entertaining are the gangly cement cowboys and Indians of **Old Trappers Lodge**. It's a strangely proportioned carnival-colored tableau of wild-west savagery that was salvaged from a demolished theme hotel and (for reasons rather mysterious) moved to parkland on the western side of Pierce College campus in Woodland Hills. There's a picnic table next to the Boothill display, so bring some egg salad and make a day of it!

Last, but by no means least, there's **Grandma Prisbrey's Bottle Village** (4595 Cochran St, Simi Valley, 805-584-0572, www.echomatic. home.mindspring.com/bv) the creation of world-class eccentric Tressa Prisbrey. It's a collection of huts, gazebos, and walkways built of cement, bottles and decorative refuse from the local dump. Originally built to house Grandma's out-of-control pencil collection, and badly damaged in the 1994 Northridge quake, the village still retains a bittersweet, slightly spooky charm. Not open to the public because of seismic damage, the Village can still be visited by appointment, or by volunteers willing to help with some (casual) cleaning or restoration. Give them a hand and have your picture taken by the bouquet of impaled dolls' heads decaying on stakes.

Now... go make some art of your own!

CHAPTER & VERSE
Literary LA
S.A. Griffin

LA is the mother of reinvention, a love song, a poem, a hungry fog, famous smog, a silicone nightmare, collagen lips the size of bumpers, traffic, arterial freeways, languages and people from every big and little place on the map. Our Lady Queen of the Angels is a place where, depending upon your mood, you can either be lost or found. A growing city with a transient skin, a lead belly and home to one of the most underappreciated and diverse group of writers on the planet.

On the concrete surface, it is easy to understand why we would have such a plethora of recognized (and unrecognized) talent, as it can be argued that truly the best and the brightest are here now. They can be found pounding away on their computer keyboards in coffeehouses, vertically integrated office towers, manic and depressed inside their overpriced digs chronicling their day-to-day from within the marrow of this transformed desert sprawl. Los Angeles is a dream factory and Mecca for the born loser. Count me in.

Nathaniel West came to LA to make rent as a screenwriter, but ended up finding his mark authoring *Day of the Locust*, the remarkable novel reflecting his brief time here as part of the entertainment machine. Ironically, the native New Yorker died at 37 in an automobile accident on his way to F. Scott Fitzgerald's funeral. Fitzgerald himself relocated here in 1937 to work as a scriptwriter and had just begun work on his own ode to corruption and the motion picture industry, *The Last Tycoon,* when he died of a heart attack at 44. Stranger than fiction?

F. Scott also figures in with writer Dorothy Parker and **the Garden of Allah**, 8152 Sunset Blvd. Ms. Parker, who lived in W. Hollywood, 8983 Norma Place, with her husband Alan, spent quality time at the notorious Garden partying with the likes of William Faulkner, Robert Benchley, F. Scott and Zelda, Ernest Hemingway and the elusive Greta Garbo. Alas, the fabulous Garden was razed in 1959 and is now reduced to a small historical marker in a parking lot lorded over by the cheeseburgers, french fries and golden arches.

Speaking of Hollywood, Jerry Stahl's early career as a television writer is well chronicled in his dark memoir, *Permanent Midnight*. Stahl recently published another novel about early Hollywood, the dream syndicate and its machinations, *I, Fatty*, a fictionalized, first person account of Mr. Arbuckle's trial for indulging in a Coke and a smile with Virginia Rappe for which he ultimately took the rap. Miss Rappe's grave, as well as those of many other silver screen luminaries, can be found at **Hollywood Forever Cemetery**

(6000 Santa Monica Blvd., Hollywood, 1888-FOREVER, www.hollywoodforever.com.).

Native Brit Christopher Isherwood resided with his partner, artist Don Bachardy, in Pacific Palisades only a mile up the road from close friend and fellow Anglo writer, Aldus Huxley. While living on Adelaide Drive, Isherwood wrote what many consider his best, *A Single Man*, chronicling the day in the life of a British professor living in Santa Monica Canyon coping with the loss of his young lover. Huxley, yet another who came to Hollywood to write for the screen, is most famous for his dystopian masterwork, *Brave New World*, and his psychedelic insights as chronicled in *The Doors of Perception*. Mr. Huxley lived here until his death on November 22, 1963, the same day that ended that one brief shining moment that was known as Camelot.

Screenwriter and novelist Hubert Selby, *Last Exit To Brooklyn* and *Requiem for a Dream*, who wrote about hard-edged life, drugs and the hustle of the Big Apple, moved his family to Los Angeles in 1967. He was back and forth for years, settling here permanently in 1983 until his passing in 2004. However, maybe the most famous non-native of writers to capture the character and essence of this enigmatic metropolis is Raymond Chandler.

Through virtuoso use of language, Chandler would forever transform Los Angeles into an unforgettable noir landscape of blinking neon, killer femmes and broken-hearted private eyes. Born in Chicago in 1888, Raymond emigrated to England at the age of seven with his divorced mother, later becoming a British citizen. In 1917, he served in the trenches of France. After the war, he became vice president of a Los Angeles oil company, only to be fired for drunkenness and absenteeism in 1932. It was during this time that Raymond Chandler found his calling as a writer of hard-boiled crime fiction and detective stories. Chandler's first novel, *The Big Sleep*, published in 1939, introduced the tough-talking, hard-drinking private dick, Philip Marlowe.

After the loss of his wife in 1954, Chandler, like a character in one of his narratives, spent the remainder of his life battling depression and alcohol, passing away in 1959. In 1994, the corner of Hollywood and Cahuenga Boulevards in the heart of Hollywood, was designated **Raymond Chandler Square**, as the location of Phillip Marlowe's fictitious 6th floor office. The place where "she" walks in, the heart skips a beat, and the music begins again. Velma...

Migrating to America from Germany with his family at the age of two, Henry Charles Bukowski — drinker, back alley brawler, postman, rooming house madrigal, dirty old man, and prolific writer — is often wrongly aligned with the Beat Generation. Yes, he was tight with Venice Beat John Thomas, nd worked the sure bet with Gerald Locklin knocking back a few at the **49er Tavern** in Long Beach (5660 E. Pacific Coast Hwy, 562-494-7670), but he was never "Beat." Post-WWII, Charles Bukowski made the scene as a one-man revolution of letters, profoundly inspiring a vast legion of imitators and the next generation of writers. A junior college drop-out, the self-taught writer attended Los Angeles City College on Vermont Ave. for about a year. His childhood home, "the chamber of horrors," was at **2122 Longwood Ave.**, LA. Other Los Angeles residences of Hank's can be found at **1623 N. Mariposa Ave., 5124 De Longpre Ave.**, and **5437¾ Carlton Way**. (Please do not disturb current occupants).

Hank dug the Mexican cuisine at **Barrigan's** (1538 Sunset Blvd.) in Echo Park, and the books at **Williams' Book Store** (443 West Sixth St., San Pedro). He could be found tipping the bottle at **Frank'n'Hank's**, (518 S. Western Ave., LA). If you really want to catch the real thing, go to Arcadia's **Santa**

Anita Race Track (285 W. Huntington Dr., Arcadia, www.santaanita.com) and drop a few bucks on Hasachance, your longshot pony might come in. You can visit Hank's gravesite at **Green Hills Memorial Park** (27051 S. Western Ave., Rancho Palos Verdes, Ocean View, Lot I, No. 875). One tough cat, Hank liked yellow poppies.

The best place to find "underground" writers and writing might be in a few bookstores and public libraries, the downtown branch of the Los Angeles Public Library being one of the most notable. **The Central Library** (630 W. Fifth St., LA, 213-228-7272, www.lapl.org) in the historic core district, was designed by Bertram Goodhue in 1926, restored and expanded in 1993. It houses a stunning array of art, artifact and murals, and is referenced in work by native Angeleno and High Priestess of Word, Wanda Coleman. This library is said to be where Charles Bukowski discovered writer John Fante. Bukowski was so taken by Fante, he sent Black Sparrow publisher John Martin a copy of *Ask The Dust* demanding republication of Fante's book as condition of further publication of his own work. Screenwriter and novelist John Fante captured Jazz Age Los Angeles forever in that classic book and in his last, *Dreams From Bunker Hill*, published before his death in 1983.

For nighthawk ambiance and grub, hit **The Original Pantry** (877 S. Figueroa St., Downtown, 213-972-9279, open 24/7). A true favorite of many writers, it is notoriously rumored that a number of the waitstaff are former convicts. (Editors' note: the owners used to routinely hire ex-cons to give them a second chance). This workingman's diner has the best ham and eggs, pancakes, cole slaw, and for the price, steaks, anywhere in LA. Order your fries from the bottom. I like to sit at the counter when I go, watch the cooks, talk with the waitstaff and carry on conversations with fellow patrons. Dig the lady in the cage that makes your change, be good to her.

Philippe's the Original (1001 N. Alameda St., LA, 213-628-3781, www.philippes.com) stands one block north of Union Station. This Art Deco masterpiece and landmark serving Angelenos since 1908, Philippe's is the *it* place for baseball, trains, and French dip, and for years was the meeting place for the Circus Club, as the Ringling Brothers trains would park at the tracks directly across the street. A few clicks from historic Olvera St. where our city began, Phillipe's is where the French Dip was born. Be warned, the hot mustard will clear your sinuses. A labyrinth of wood benches and booths, John Gilmore and Ron Kenner wrote part of their novel, *Garbage People: The Trip to Helter-Skelter and Beyond with Charlie Manson and The Family* here.

Raymond Chandler's old hangout, **The Pacific Dining Car** (1310 W. 6th St., LA, 213-483-6000, www.pacificdining car.com), moved in 1923 to its present location. Originally at 7th and Westlake, the world-class restaurant is a lifelong favorite of LA native and master mystery writer, James Ellroy. Mr. Ellroy first experienced the restaurant on his tenth birthday with his father and later in life would marry his second wife, Helen Knode, here. Vikram Jayanti's *James Ellroy's Feast of Death*, a feature documentary about the famous crime writer, is laced with meals at the Pacific Dining Car throughout. In a number of scenes Ellroy, cops and Nick Nolte discuss the infamous Black Dahlia murder and the killing of Ellroy's mother. Ellroy also included the restaurant in *L.A. Confidential*.

Frequented by the hoi polloi, natives and tourists, **Musso & Frank's** (6667 Hollywood Blvd., Hollywood, 323-467-7788) is the oldest restaurant in Hollywood. Operating since 1919, the establishment is notorious for their dry martinis, steaks, lobster and a litany of famous and infamous literary regulars. The back room, closed since the 1950s, was where writers William Saroyan, Dorothy Parker, and many others ate, drank and made merry. To this day, celebrity writers hold court and dine here.

Musso's was also a big favorite of Charles Bukowski. He and good pal Red Stodolsky, who owned **Baroque Books**, dined here often. When I first went on the hunt for anything Bukowski, Red was the man. Red befriended many famous and not so famous writers as a bookseller, including Henry Miller. Sadly, nothing remains of the landmark bookstore at 1643 North Las Palmas Ave., just south of Hollywood Blvd. It'd be nice if there was a plaque outside that said, "Books slept here."

A hangout for journalists, beatniks, pop artists, poets and rock stars, **Barney's Beanery** (447 Santa Monica Blvd, W. Hollywood, 323-654-5123, www.barneysbeanery.com) opened its doors in 1920, finding its present location in 1927. Part eatery, juke joint, poolhall and bar, The Beanery is one of the longest-standing roadhouses on Route 66, and the third oldest restaurant in LA. In 1945, *Hollywood Nightlife* magazine said, "Barney Anthony is a name known to most writers who at one time or another have been broke in this town. Barney has always made sure that they have had food and just a little cash to tide them over." Quentin Tarantino wrote much of *Pulp Fiction* sitting in his favorite booth. Barney's was a very popular hang for the Semina Gang which included Wallace Berman, John Altoon, Jay de Feo and Dennis Hopper.

Located in historic **Liemert Park**, the **World Stage** (4344 Degnan Blvd., between 43rd St. and 43rd Place, 323-293-2451, www.theworldstage.org/lit.html) is home to one of the best word happenings in Southern California. Founded in 1989 by the late, great jazz drummer Billy Higgins and master poet and community activist Kamau Daáood, the Anansi Writer's

Workshop at World Stage has a stunning history of music and lit, holding open and featured readings on Wednesday nights. I cannot recommend this series highly enough. And dig this, there are also damned hot word scenes across the street at the new **Fifth Street Dicks**, hosted by Deep Red and A.K. Toney.

The Los Angeles Science Fiction Club, whose membership includes Ray Bradbury, Robert Heinlein, and L. Ron Hubbard, first met in the **Pacific Electric Building** at **Cole's Pacific Electric Buffet** (118 E. 6th St., www.colespebuffet.com/dtown.html, 213-622-4090). Designed by architect Thornton Fitzhugh in a Beaux Arts style, The Pacific Electric, completed by Henry Huntington in 1905, was the city's first skyscraper, and remained the tallest building west of Chicago until the 1950s. The famous Red Line transit system actually emanated from the ground floor of the building to service the entire Los Angeles sprawl facilitating future growth. For my money, Cole's, operating inside the building since 1908, has the best hot pastrami in LA (also alleged to have been invented here), and sports one of the finest and funkiest old-school bars in the city. Cole's hosts many an underground event with music, poets and writers in the intensely rich back room. Eight floors up from the buffet — in complete contrast — the ultra-exclusive Jonathan Club held court. Later, the LASFC would move their meetings close by to another Los Angeles landmark, **Clifton's Brookdale Cafeteria** (648 S. Broadway, 213-627-1673, www.cliftonscafeteria.com).

Al's Bar (305 S. Hewitt St.) raged at the bottom floor of the **American Hotel** for 20 years. Always the most Beat, beaten and best bohemian hang in Los Angeles, Al's was genuinely punk from the very first day. Writers, artists and musical folk from every walk and school lost their minds and found their hearts here, all sadly gone.

Black Ace Books in Silver Lake (323-661-5052, www.blackace.net) has a long, rich history that begins in Denver with Venice Beats Tony Scibella, Steve Wilson and Stuart Z. Perkoff. During the punk '80s, Black Ace operated across the street from Hollywood High. Ultimately it landed at its present home with partners Rose Idlet and Scibella in the spring of 1990. Tony passed on in October of 2004, and the store has since been Rose's baby, open only by telephone or mail appointments. The catalog includes vintage paperbacks: sleaze, mystery, detective, juvenile delinquent, science fiction, fantasy, and westerns. This place is a treasure.

Mother Road **Route 66** literally meets land's end at the Santa Monica Pier and Boardwalk, just north of **Venice Beach**. Venice Beach is where you will find the three **Poet's Walls** — one by the police station, one by the public pissers, and the third by the public showers, of course! Read the poetry of Jim Morrison, Viggo Mortensen, Amy Gertzler and others.

The Venice Beats inhabited the slum-by-the-surf for a brief but stormy period between about 1957-62 and were made famous on the cover of *Life* magazine and in the pages of *The Holy Barbarians* by Lawrence Lipton. The old **Venice West Café** (7 Dudley Ave.) established by poet Stuart Z. Perkoff is now **Sponto Gallery** (310-245-4882), where the Beat goes on with readings, film events and art. The other infamous Venice Beat hangout, **The Gas House,** (1501 Ocean Front Walk), just south of Market Street, was razed in 1962 and is now, literally, just a pillar.

A funny and insightful period piece and mind movie recollection by poet and Gas House chef John Thomas and Venice Poet Laureate Philomene Long, *Bukowski in the Bathtub* is partially taken from tape recordings made by Thomas at his Echo Park digs back when Hank and John were tight from 1965-71. In Beat speak, Tony Scibella once told me that the reason they all snapped their fingers wasn't to be cool, but to keep the cops away. Noise laws, baby! Like, wow, what a king-sized drag.

Beyond Baroque Literary Arts Center (681 Venice Blvd., www.beyondbaroque.com, 310-822-3006) is where the Wednesday night poetry workshop, founded in 1969 by Joseph Hansen and Papa Bach Bookstore legend John Harris, still leads the First Amendment chorus. The historic, long-running workshop has been helmed by some of the finest poets and writers in Los Angeles including Bob Flanagan and Frank T. Rios. Baroque is notorious for being the meeting place of punk progenitors Exene Cervenka and John Doe, and over time has become a Who's Who of poets and writers like Kate Braverman, Dennis Cooper, Benjamin Wiessman, Laurel Ann Bogen, Wanda Coleman, Richard Meltzer, and LA punk legend, Screamers singer Tomata du Plenty. Beyond Baroque also houses the best alternative and small press poetry bookstore anywhere in LA.

Down in the San Fernando Valley, at the **Cobalt Café** (22047 Sherman Way, Canoga Park) www.cobaltcafe.com/history, 818-348-3789), Superhighwayman Rick Lupert has been hosting one of the best open mikes and featured readings on Tuesday nights since 1994.

Once Brentwood Bookshop, **Dutton's Books** (11975 San Vicente Blvd., Brentwood, 310-476-6263, www.duttons brentwood.com) began operating in October of 1984, and has established itself as one of the best independent bookstores in the country. Dutton's stocks best-sellers and popular titles, music, philosophy, has its own café, courtyard and an incredible selection of poetry titles. Dogs welcome: have Spot bark for poet/employee Scott Wannberg and he will give your literary canine a doggie biscuit! Over the years, Dutton's has always been staffed by writers, including award-winning novelist Diane Leslie.

Still a true alternative, **Skylight Books** in hipster Los Feliz (1818 N. Vermont Ave., 323-660-1175) is another fine independent bookstore staffed by writers and poets. Occupying the same space left empty by **Chatterton's Books**, Skylight has its strengths in literary fiction, cinema, books on Los Angeles, poetry, and alternative literature. Relax and read under the branches of the huge ficus tree growing right in the middle of the store! Say hi to Lucy when you're there, she's the store's orange Tabby.

Just down the block at 1802 N. Vermont Ave. was **the Onyx Café**. Writers of every ilk, slackers, bohemians, punks, junkies, drunks, artists, musicians, and coffee fanatics used to congregate here non-stop, until popular culture and real estate drove everyone out. Poet Steve Abee worked here, Beck sat in on readings with his guitar pre-"Loser." The spot is now a French Bistro, of course. Vive Le Onyx!

For the real alternative, **Koma Books** (814 S. La Brea Ave., 213-622-0501, www.komabookstore.com,) is the shit. The titles they carry will freak the ordinary reader, but thrill the freaks! Find work by acclaimed author and native son John Gilmore, Warhol superstar Mary Woronov, and LA-based publisher Feral House. Sleaze, neuropolitics, mayhem, control/anarchy, and exotica all found here.

What you have experienced on this very brief poet's tour really does only scratch the very surface of this amazing city. If you want to know LA, its writers, or anything about it... live in it, love the city and its people. Don't waste your breath talking the city down, it is a moot exercise in rabidly cliché behavior. And remember, as Bukowski is famous for saying, "You're only a writer when you are writing... don't try."

YOU LOOK LIKE A MOVIE STAR, HONEY
Karen Cusolito

One of the joys of vacationing is getting your hair cut in a strange city. Okay, it may not compare to sex in a strange city, but sometimes you have to take your joys where you can find them. Vacations give you the perfect excuse for cheating on your stylist: "I was out of town and desperately needed a cut. What could I do?" Fortunately, there are plenty of good stylists in Los Angeles. One search engine listed 2,429. I think I've been to at least half of those in the last 20 years, and I've never gotten a bad cut (color is another story).

My current fave is **Lucas** (1541 Echo Park Ave., 213-250-7992, lucasechopark.com), a laid-back salon that offers cuts, color, waxing, and facials in an artsy yet ungentrified neighborhood near Dodger Stadium. Cuts are $75 and one-hour facials are $65. Three doors down from the salon, owner

Taylor Lucas's sister Nina runs an annex where you can get your nails done and shop for her signature line of clothes. In between are art galleries and vintage clothing stores. Once a month, the various proprietors have a block party where local artists show their new work. Each business gets involved, setting out beer or wine while locals take in the scene. Before you leave the neighborhood, have a taco or burrito at one of the street stands and find out why Los Angeles has better Mexican food than Mexico.

If you are Eastside-phobic, or you absolutely must tell the folks back home that you got your hair cut in Beverly Hills, you don't have to pay the $200+ that some top salons charge. At **Vidal Sassoon** (9403 Santa Monica Blvd., Beverly Hills, 310-274-8791) you can have your hair cut by a stylist-in-training for less than the cost of a parking ticket. These assistants cut both men's and women's hair for $17, using one of the 24 cuts Sassoon teaches. Single color is $25. An instructor checks their work.

Another low-cost, high-style alternative is **Rudy's Barbershop** (8300 W. Sunset Blvd., 323-650-5669; 4451 W. Sunset Blvd., 323-661-6535). There are no appointments, but you can call ahead and put your name on a list to shorten the wait time. Buzz cuts are $19 and fashion cuts are $26. The Silver Lake location is in a converted garage, while the Hollywood location is inside The Standard hotel, a good place to get a drink and take in the sights while you wait.

MARTINIS AND MANICURES

Speaking of drinks, you can tip one back *and* get a manicure during happy hour at **Beauty Bar** (1638 N. Cahuenga Blvd., 323-464-767, beautybar.com). If Patsy and Edina were to visit LA, this is where you'd find them. The bar, designed like a 1960s beauty salon, offers free manicures or henna tattoos from 6-11 p.m. Thursdays through Sundays, when you buy a $10 "Prell," "Shampoo," "Platinum Blonde," or any other drink.

Wednesday is Champagne Wednesday at **la vie l'orange**, (638 1/2 N. Robertson Blvd., LA, 310-289-2501, www.lavie lorange.com), although a manicurist told me, "Cosmos, margaritas, whatever you want." The spa says it is a chemical-free environment that only uses natural-based products, including their signature cucumber-orange scent. This is one of Oprah's favorite spots, and the day I was there, Nicole Richie and friends were getting a pedicure and mouthing off for MTV's *The Surreal Life*. (The conversation turned to vaginal rejuvenation, with Richie exclaiming, "You don't want a wrinkly box or your husband will leave you.") Surreal indeed. A basic mani-pedi is $50. They also offer reflexology, brow shaping, facial waxing, and makeup application. The spa is open every day but Monday. On days other than Wednesday, you'll be offered tea, coffee or a glass of red or white wine.

If you prefer your manicures sober, there are a myriad of options, from fancy-schmancy spas to cheapie shops in nearly every strip mall. Nail shops outnumber donut shops or liquor stores in many neighborhoods. For awesome airbrush designs, go to **CT Nails III** (7868 Santa Monica Blvd. at Fairfax, West Hollywood, 323-656-6189) for $15 for a full set, or $3 a nail. A mani-pedi is $18.

SNEAKS AND STRIPPER SHOES

Now that you're looking good from your head to your feet, it's time to go shopping. Show off those toes with a new pair of shoes. For stripper style, try any number of shops on Hollywood Boulevard east of Highland Avenue, near Wilcox. Looking for the coolest sneakers? **Blu-82** (2025 Sawtelle Blvd., LA, 310-445-0909) is the new store form Jisook Lee, who owns clothing store **Black Market** (310-966-1555) next door. The clothing store has modern Japanese style, and odd items like Nippies Patch of Freedom "for that seductress who doesn't like to wear bras under her sheers. Reusable and waterproof $16." The shoestore stocks PF Flyers, Creative Recreation, and Le Coq Sportif. While you're in the neighborhood, have a bite to eat at one of the noodle shops or the Japanese grocery store.

What happens when your favorite pair of shoes experiences wardrobe malfunction? Stop by **Willie's Shoe Repair**, (801 N. Cahuenga Blvd. 323-463-5011) across the street from Ren-Mar Studios. Wilebaldo Rivera is the shoe-repairer to the stars. His shop is decorated with dusty photos of Ava Gardner, Michael Douglas, and Placido Domingo, among others, who have signed their photos with personal notes to Willie. He also makes customs and rebuilt shoes.

OUTLETS AND SAMPLE SALES

There are tons of places with the word "outlet" in the name, but buyer beware, it's usually just a euphemism for junk. One exception is the **Circle Indie Designer Outlet**, (2395 Glendale Blvd., LA, 323-665-5336, open seven days, noon-7 p.m.). They have tops, bottoms, dresses, some baby items, jewelry and sunglasses from such Los Angeles designers as Mon Petit Oiseau, Trina Turk, Grey Ant, Lockets, Burning Torch, and Monah Li. Another local designer, **Maggie Barry** (1734 Silver Lake Blvd., LA, 323-663-9526) sells samples of her sexy tops and dresses that manage to reveal your assets and conceal your liabilities. She does a lot of styles in stretch jersey. Open Wednesday through Sunday, "or whenever you see the doors open," she says.

Los Angeles is a great town for samples sales; there's usually more than one going one every weekend. **Sassy City**

Chicks (www.sassycitychicks.com) holds sample sales that includes such designers as La Bijou Belle, Ana Capri, Krisa, Bloom Designs, Samora Designs, Moss Mills Design, Anna Beck Designs, Rio Rags. **Daily Candy** and **LA.Com** lists sample sales on their e-mailing lists. Go online to sign up.

DRAG QUEENS AND NATURE GIRLS

Ball Beauty Supply (416 N. Fairfax Ave., 323-655-2330), across the street from **Canter's Deli**, is a treasure-trove for drag queens and glamour pusses. There's a stunning assortment of false eyelashes, a rack of moustache wax, silver hair clips for holding yamulkes in place, and après-shampoo turbans priced from $7.95 to $13.95.

If you are more of a natural beauty, we've got that covered too. Before **Whole Foods Market** sprouted throughout Los Angeles, there was **Erewhon** (7660 Beverly Blvd., 323-937-0777) for your homeopathic remedies and natural hair dye. It's also a good choice for a cheap meal or snack to fuel your shopping.

On Sunday, walk (yes, we do walk occasionally) down Ivar between Sunset and Hollywood boulevards for the **Hollywood Farmers Market** (9 a.m. to 3 p.m.) You'll find fresh flowers, espresso, tamales, bread, and other edibles, as well as funky arts and crafts. On Saturday, the **Silver Lake Farmers Market** (Sunset Boulevard at Maltman, 9 a.m. to 1 p.m.) has similar items in a smaller area.

A short drive (or a long walk) down Sunset takes you past the thriving Silver Lake shopping circuit. Check out the one-of-a-kind shops offering everything from handmade soap to tattoos. When you reach Virgil, you'll find **Uncle Jer's** (4459 Sunset Blvd., 323-662-6710). It's a neighborhood landmark that has been donating a portion of its profits to humanitarian causes since before it was fashionable. In addition to colorful, ethnic clothes, there's fun stuff like plastic rings with bugs in them, and cards featuring photos of Los Angeles.

Down the street, where Hollywood Boulevard begins, is **Ozzie Dots** (4637 Hollywood Blvd., 323-663-2867) where there's a line down the block come Halloween. It's the go-to spot for costumes, but it also has a year-round selection of vintage clothing, purses, hats, gloves, belts, and clown makeup.

BARGAIN SHOPPING

For real cha-cha fashion, head east to **Fashions of Echo Park** (1600 W. Sunset Blvd., 213-482-723) or **Fashions for Eva** (1557 W. Sunset Blvd., 213-250-2526). Both are open daily and stock such must-have items as 99-cent nail polish and lipstick, $2.99 stick-on bras, extremely inexpensive trendy club wear, fishnet stockings and animal-print underwear.

The real Mecca for bargain hunters is **Santee Alley** in the **Garment District,** Downtown LA (Santee Street between Maple Street and Olympic Boulevard, open daily) where you'll find the cheapest knock-offs of whatever is in style at the moment, including clothes, shoes, accessories, and kids clothing. If all that shopping whips up a mean appetite, stop at **The Original Pantry** (877 S. Figueroa, 213-972-9279), former Mayor Richard Riordan's landmark eatery that's open 24/7. Carnivores will enjoy the steaks and chops, sure to produce shrieks of horror from vegans.

Bollywood style can be found in a number of places, but for the real deal, visit the **Little India** neighborhood in Artesia (Pioneer Boulevard between 183rd and 187th Street), 20 miles southeast of downtown Los Angeles. It's 20-30 minutes by car, but a world away in imagination. These roughly four blocks contain nearly everything an Indiaphile could wish for, including jeweled bindis, Banghara CDs, and thousands of current and vintage Bollywood flicks. **India Sari Palace**

(18640 S. Pioneer Blvd., Artesia, 562-402-7939) sells silk saris and tie-dyed cotton tops. **Cottage Art** (18619 S. Pioneer Blvd., Artesia, www.cottageart.com) stocks everything from clothing to books, household items, and ayurvedic skin care. Sets of beaded and bangled bracelets sell for $7.90 and ankle bracelets are $3.90.

GLAMAZONS

Most boutiques carry lingerie for normal-size gals. A good source is **Panty Raid** (2378-1/2 Glendale Blvd., LA, 323-668-1888) which sells Cosabella, Felina, and Hanky Panky. But buxom babes have a harder time; when they do find something in their size, there's usually a shortage of selection. Follow the yellow brick road to the **Wizard of Bras** (1530 Myrtle Ave., Monrovia, www.wizardofbras.com) which has specialized in fitting well-endowed women since 1975. Exit the 210 Freeway at Myrtle and look for the King Kong-sized bra in the window. (You'll see it a block away.) Inside the front room is a curious collection of cheesy babydolls, seamed pantyhose, and condoms disguised as lollipops. But step into the hallway and put your name down on a wait list for a fitting. While you wait, you can browse the swimsuits in cup sizes of FF, GG, and H. When it's your turn, you'll pass through the swinging doors into a back room where a saleswoman will measure you and bring out a tub of brassieres in your size. Makers include Felina, Jezebel, Lunaire, Glamorise, Prima Donna, and Goddess in sizes up to JJ. They ship worldwide with no handling fees. Best bet: go on a weekday. Saturday afternoon can be a zoo. Closed Sunday.

Continue the kitsch vibe by visiting one of the great tiki bars in the Southland: **Bahooka** (4501 N. Rosemead Blvd., Rosemead, 626-285-1241, www.bahooka.com, open daily until 9 p.m., 11 p.m. on Friday and Saturday). It's about five miles away, but it will be on your way back to Los Angeles. Inside the carved wooden doors, the first thing you see is Rufus, a 27-year-old Pacu fish who eats carrots. The next thing you see will be hundreds of fish tanks. Fish tanks at the bar, behind the bar, next to nearly every table. Two can share a flaming Bahooka Bowl (vodka) or Honey Bowl (rum), which comes in a salad bowl with two long straws, $18. Just make sure your designated driver can make it back to Los Angeles in one piece. You'd hate to end a perfect day in the hoosegow. Even Patsy and Edina would have a hard time getting out of that.

L.A. VICE
Iris Berry

Okay, so you wanna get high, you wanna get low, you wanna get down and you need to get sideways, and you gotta go uptown to go "Downtown," you wanna Chase the Dragon, you wanna chase the store clerk, and you're gonna get chased by the cops on the 5 o'clock news. You gotta get screwed and tattooed, laid and paid, tied up and beat up. You're gonna get your freak on and you need to get your tweak on... or all of the above and you don't know where to go! Well, being a huge former fan and an avid participant of the life of vice, I've been chewed up and spit out a few times by our pretty city's underbelly, and somehow, luckily, lived to tell. So, here are a few places that might get you what you're looking for, but *be very careful*, not recommended for the weak at heart or the perenially stupid. We will not be held responsible for your use of the information provided here. If you're doing something on the down-low, be cool and DON'T GET CAUGHT!

SEX SHOPS

The Pleasure Chest (7733 Santa Monica Blvd., West Hollywood, 323-650-1022, thepleasure chest.com) True to its name, since 1975, the Pleasure Chest has helped pioneer the Sexual Revolution with the launch of the original sex toy "boutique." Over three decades later, the Pleasure Chest has locations across America and has been featured in HBO's *Sex and the City* making the Rabbit vibrator an overnight sensation! They have a huge selection of sex games, sexy treats, bachelorette party essentials, sexy sweets, sex toys, dildos, vibrators, strap-ons, lubricants, men's sex toys, bachelor party supplies, books and movies... is it getting hot in here, or is it just me? Wheeew! You name it they got it.

Hustler Hollywood (8920 Sunset Blvd., West Hollywood, 310-860-9009, HustlerHollywood.com) Fortunately, going to a sex shop these days doesn't have to be the dark and sleazy experience it used to be (although some may prefer that). Nowadays, with a sex shop like the sun-lit Hustler Store, buying sex toys, adult DVDs, and lingerie can feel as casual as going to the make-up counter at Bloomingdale's. Rumor has it that Teresa Flynt, daughter of *Hustler* magazine maven Larry Flynt, is the manager of Hustler Hollywood. The store has everything you need to become a porn star, except a tanning booth. With one-size-fits-surgically-altered, the store is conveniently located in West Hollywood on the fabulous Sunset Strip, and even has a yummy coffee bar with sidewalk seating. So feel free to have your coffee drink, relax and enjoy the view, both inside and out of the store, and maybe even catch a glimpse of legendary porn stars browsing the aisles.

SMOKE SHOPS

We used to call them "head shops" until the 1980s when terminology laws came into existence, and what we called "paraphernalia" had to change in order to keep the stores open. Now we call them "Smoke shops," we don't call them "bongs," we call them "water pipes," etc, etc... You catchin' my drift?

Captain Ed's (6704 Van Nuys Blvd., Van Nuys, 818-989-3222; also 7011 Reseda Blvd, Reseda, 818-996-1222) Originally called Heads'n'High's in the 1960s. Captain Ed's is a landmark on the famous Van Nuys Blvd. The oldest of its kind established in 1967. This place is packed with water pipes (not "bongs," right?), blacklight posters, marijuana patches of all shapes and sizes, can safes, and basically every smoking accessory you've ever heard of. It's chock full of all '60s and '70s memorabilia, and stays true to form with Pink Floyd and the Grateful Dead blasting over the sound system. An original and a classic. They don't make them like this anymore. You can feel the spirit of R. Crumb and Jerry Garcia as you walk in the door... and ask for Chris, he's awesome!

Chronic Creations Smoke Shop (1600 Main St., Venice., 310-821-6299) The finest in hand-blown glass smoking accessories. Upscale and jaw-dropping merchandise. For the smoker who has everything.

STRIP CLUBS

Jumbo's Clown Room (5153 Hollywood Blvd., Hollywood, 323-666-118, www.jumbos.com) Known far and wide by the rock n' roll locals and anyone in-the-know when coming through town on tour. Just your average, down-home, mom and pop, neighborhood, rock n' roll, bikini bar. Located in a tiny Hollywood strip mall. Small and quaint and anything but corporate since 1982. It was in 1986 that Jumbos was really put on the map, when Courtney Love graced their humble stage with her charms. This place beats the hell out of Hooters, that's for sure.

Cheetah's (4600 Hollywood Blvd, LA, 323-660-6733) is a bikini bar with a big screen tv, a pool table and a full bar. One of my favorite strip joints in LA. Not your mama's strip club, a lot of the girls are tattooed and more on edgy side... and super cute! They're not your average corporate cookie-cutter stripper-types.

Spearmint Rhino Gentlemen's Club (630 Maulhardt Ave., Oxnard, 805-988-6518, www.spearmintrhino.com) Now this is your serious corporate stripclub chain. Upscale and worldwide, since 1989 with over 30 locations. Their website boasts of entertainment and shows including adult film star performances on a regular basis. Hours are: Sunday - Thursday,11-2am. Friday & Saturday: 11-4am. Admission: before 6:30 pm $5, 6:30 pm-Close $20. Strictly nude, no alcohol served. Must be 18+ to enter. Dress code enforced. Conveniently, just off the "Ho Stro," otherwise known as Sepulveda Boulevard in Van Nuys.

TATTOO PARLORS

Spotlight Tattoo (5859 Melrose Ave., 323-871-1084, www.spotlighttattoo.com, call for appointment) Owned and operated by Bob Roberts, tattoo legend. Not only is Bob an amazing tattoo artist, but a phenomenal saxophone player as well. He's played with Frank Zappa, Hot Tuna, and the New York Dolls, to name a few. You can probably hear some really amazing stories while getting your ink. So why just let anyone tattoo you when you can have a legendary tattoo from Bob Roberts?

Mark Mahoney's Shamrock Social Club (9026 W Sunset Blvd., West Hollywood, 310-271-9664) And while we're on the subject of legendary tattoos, Mark Mahoney is not only legendary but he's drop-dead gorgeous! Who cares what he's saying while giving you your legendary ink, he's just niiiice to look at. And for you guys, he's also really cool and could probably teach you a thing or two, (what he forgot, you'll never know) and if anything, having one of Mark's tattoos on you *will* impress the ladies. And if Mark's too booked, ask for Mike Roach, (also real easy on the eyes) who's not just a legendary babe and ink slinger, he also plays bass for TSOL.

American Electric Tattoo (3532 W. Sunset, 323-664-6530, www.americanelectrictattoo.com) Craig Jackman, the owner of this fine establishment is not only a damn amazing tattoo artist he also plays washboard for that crazy/fun psychobilly band, Throw Rag. (Come to think of it, he's also pretty cute) He's conveniently located in Silver Lake just a couple of doors down from **Millie's,** the renowned, bohemian, punk-rock greasy spoon that everyone and their mother worked at, myself included!

PLACES TO COP DRUGS

To score over-the-counter marijuana legally, see the Medical Marijuana info in the 'Health' chapter.

Sepulveda Boulevard also known as the "Ho Stro." Just follow the sound of sirens. From Ventura Blvd to Roscoe Blvd. Picture one long sprawling stretch of cheap motels, hookers, pimps, drug dealers, drug addicts, cops, paramedics and fire trucks. Throw in a few 7/11s, a split-level Target, a couple of gas stations, some lonely liquor stores, a few scary-ass donut shops, and maybe a carwash or two, and you've got Sepulveda Blvd., in all its gory glory. It's a drug addict's carnival, and a 24-hour affair at that. You can get anything and I do mean A-N-Y-T-H-I-N-G at a low cost on this street of broken spleens. If Section 8 crack motels is your bag, this is the place for you.

Located in the San Fernando Valley just off the 405 Freeway at the Burbank Blvd. exit. You'll know it by the trail of used condoms and ambulance lights, and beware of aggressive window washers.

MacArthur Park is melting in the dark, and someone's left the crack out in the rain. Can you say "sick" in Spanish? Cuz if you wanna go shopping down at the Park, sick, black and white… is pretty much what you'll need to know in your best carwash Spanish to navigate this open-air black market. It's open 24 hours a day, 7 days a week, it's never closed! Earthquakes, riots, Cinco de Mayo, Christmas and Chanukah, even on 9/11, the drugs were a flowin'. It's a beautiful setting, and no matter how much the city tries to gentrify it and make it nicey-nice, the drug business never seems to go away. It's an Old Faithful of a drug stop. Not only can you get drugs, but you can get a whole new identity in the form of counterfeit green cards and driver's licenses, among other things. Located at the corner of 6th and Alvarado, conveniently across the street from **Langer's Delicatessen**. So enjoy some delicious matzo ball soup while waiting for your crack cocaine. Be careful at night, the park tends to eat people. And FYI, "sick" in Spanish is "infermo."

BAIL BONDS

Allstate Bail Bonds (18750 Crenshaw Blvd. Torrance, 310-327-0950, allstatebailbonds.com) How crazy is it that this place is run by some of the '80s most sickest party animals? Bondsmen Chris Bailey and Billy Persons (formerly of the Gun Club) were heavily involved in the punk rock faux lodge loosely based on the Flintstones: The Loyal Order Of Water Buffaloes. Their meetings were legendary in drunken debauchery, and members included Keith Morris of the Circle Jerks, as well as members of The Red Hot Chili Peppers,

TSOL, Fishbone and now-famous director Gore Verbinski. In fact, to a select few, Chris still retains his title of Grand Poobah! I'm not kidding, check it out at www.loyalorderofthewaterbuffalo.com.

Bad Boys Bail Bonds, Inc. (1-800-BAIL-OUT, www.badboysbailbonds.com) Sorry, we don't know anything about these guys sordid pasts, but we're sure they can get you out of jail.

Hollywood Bail Bonds (1027 Cole Ave., 323-464-8484) See above.

TOW YARDS

Hollywood Tow (1015 N. Mansfield Ave., 323-466-5421, www.hollywoodtow.com) I like how if you go to their website, they have a mission statement about their dedication to excellence. Like we give a *rat's ass,* just give us our freakin' cars back. "Great, my car is towed, excellent!" Fuck You!

Viertel's Towing Service (500 Center St, LA, 213-687-1003) Same to you guys (see above).

REHAB AND TREATMENT CENTERS

For those of you who found yourselves needing info from the bail bonds section, some of the following numbers may also be extremely helpful to you... I'm not sayin'... I'm just sayin'!

Tarzana Treatment Center (18646 Oxnard St. Tarzana, 800-996-1051, www.tarzanatc.org)

Cry-Help Treatment Center (11027 Burbank Blvd., North Hollywood, 818-985-8323)

Promises Treatment Center 800-595-8779

Alcoholic Anonymous 323-936-4343

Narcotics Anonymous 323-933-5395

PUNK L.A.
Ryan Leach

VENUES

The Scene (806 E. Colorado Blvd., Glendale, 818-241-7029, www.thescenebar.com) The Scene has really come around thanks to the promoting work of the Guilty Hearts' Leon Catfish and Edgar Rodriguez. In the past year, the venue has hosted shows by the Lost Sounds, the Deadly Snakes, the Reatards, the Black Lips, etc. It's become a home away from home and the only venue I truly L-U-V right now.

The Smell (247 S. Main St., LA, www.thesmell.org) A philanthropic, all-ages venue. I think the guy who runs it is named Jim. Kudos to him for giving the kids a chance to see bands most places with strict age restrictions won't. Also, my buddy Kat Jetson deserves a big pat on the back for promoting countless shows here. Kat's been a workhorse and has often paid bands out of her own pocket. The sound at the Smell might not be the best, but whatever. If you go here, have some respect so the place stays open.

The Silver Lake Lounge (2906 Sunset Blvd., Silver Lake, 323-666-2407, www.foldsilverlake.com) This place is really fucking random. Some nights it'll have great punk bands; other nights you'll roll up to mariachi music and some dude in a ten-gallon hat trying to grab your dick. The beer here is expensive (come to think of it, all beer at bars is expensive), so make sure you bring your own and imbibe in the back alley (a liquor store is right across the street). REMINDER: check show dates or your ass will regret it.

The Echo (1822 Sunset Blvd., Echo Park, 213-413-8200 www.attheecho.com) I saw the Fall and Mike Watt here. In short: the Echo often rules.

Spaceland (1717 Silver Lake Blvd., Silver Lake, 323-661-4380, www.clubspaceland.com) I guess this place is beat. I don't know cause I don't really go here. It was the "hot spot" for a long time – even getting coverage in *Spin* concerning a Karen O sighting (wow!). Beck used to play here blah, blah, blah. Sometimes this place comes through. I'm ambivalent. A majority of the time a shitty band like the Blood Arm plays Spaceland, but try your luck sometime. A definite perk is the 7-11 within easy walking distance.

Zen Sushi (2609 Hyperion Ave., Silver Lake, 323-979-3869 www.zensushila.com) Fuck this place. Yeah, once in a blue moon a great band will play here, but for the most part, fuck it. I don't like the security here. It's a generality: some of the people (maybe even some of the security guards) are okay, but a good many are douche bags (the kind of douche bags who ate a lot of red meat and picked on you in high school). The douche bags ruin it for the others and the atmosphere sucks.

The Troubadour (9081 Santa Monica Blvd., West Hollywood, 310-276-6168 www.troubadour.com) This place used to hold shows for the Byrds (yes, Gene Clark was a genius) and Jackson Browne (and, yes, Jackson Browne was writing songs and having sex with Nico in the mid/late '60s.) AND SO YOU KNOW, Tom Waits fought Nickey Beat here in '78, ending punk shows at the Troubadour for a few years. The Troubadour is a bonafide venue, meaning it sucks. Seldom does a great band play here nowadays (the exception being the Reigning Sound show last year). You can squeeze about two worthwhile shows outta here a year, tops.

The Whisky (8901 Sunset Blvd, West Hollywood, 310-652-4202, www.whiskyagogo.com) For the love of God, Allah, etc., never go here, unless you come strapped with C-4 explosive. The Whisky is a dying dinosaur. It's a pay-to-play shitfest every night now. Yeah, I know, the Byrds, the Doors, X, the Minutemen and your mother used to play here, but that doesn't mean shit. Fuck the Whisky. It's an embarrassment to its former self.

The Sunset Strip If you like Hummer limos, fake boobs, shaved chests, cocaine (you supplying it), silk T-shirts, the band Creed, and have excess money to burn, you'll probably fit right in. Again, the **Key Club** is where they filmed *Night At the Roxbury* (need I say more?). Avoid this place like the plague. (Editors' note: *Night at the Roxbury* was filmed at **The Roxbury**, a club that no longer exists. The Key Club used to be **Gazzari's**, a late '80s hair-farmin' lair that spawned, like, the entire Sunset Strip Culture just mentioned: Axxel Rose and Brett Michaels wannabes, stuffed leatherette pants, etc.)

BANDS TO CHECK OUT

Fortune's Flesh (www.fortunesflesh.com): Fortune's Flesh is a continuation of the Starvations. Formed in 1999, the Starvations quickly went from a mediocre roots-punk band loaded with promise to one of the best bands Los Angeles has seen in decades (for proof, check out 2003's *Get Well Soon* and 2005's *Gravity's a Bitch*).

The Lipstick Pickups (lipstickpickups.com): The Pickups play solid, Buzzcocks-influenced punk with the quirky, teenage playfulness of Alex Chilton The band shines in the idiosyncratic vocals of Tracey, who sounds like Pete Shelly imitating a chipmunk. This makes the Pickups endearing to some, loathsome to others. Highlights include a song on 2002's *Let's Get Rid of LA* compilation and a few solid singles for **Kapow Records** (www.kapow records.com).

The Checkers (www.thecheckers.net): The Checkers is another *Let's Get Rid of LA* band who's just released its second full-length, *Running With Scissors* (www.teenacide records.com). Definitely underrated, this new wave inspired act excels: fans of Blondie, take heed.

The Guilty Hearts (www.redonfire.com/theguiltyhearts/): These boys have been fucking up the blues like good old Jeffrey Lee Pierce used to. Rabid audiophiles, the guys mix *Fire of Love* era Gun Club with the two guitars, no bass assault of the Oblivions (does it get any better?). Throw in Los Angeles punk legend Hermann Senac on drums, and you have a sound as deadly as the stock market crash of '29.

The Flash Express come equipped with all the self-boasting and diatribes you'd expect from LA's answer to the James Brown Show. The band's a throwback to a time when emphasis was put on making every show a memorable one; certainly STAX live shows come to mind, not to mention the Flash Express' strong, MG's-like rhythm section. There is only one Flash Express. LA's lucky to have it.

Almighty Do Me a Favor (almighty domeafavor.com): Almighty Do Me a Favor is Bradley Williams. Bradley is a one man band cut from the same cloth as his mentor, Hazel Adkins. Bradley switches from guitar to banjo, from California to Alabama, as often as he feels. He shows up to LA unexpectedly, leaves unexpectedly, plays parks and parking lots at the drop of a dime, etc. He's the most punk person I know. Check out his Kapow (www.kapowrecords.com) 45 entitled *Won't be None*.

The Rolling Blackouts (rollingblackouts.com): The Rolling Blackouts sounds like its from Detroit, but thank God the band's from LA. The Blackouts have a record out on Record Collection (recordcollectionmusic.com), *Black is Beautiful*.

The Red Onions (www.theredonions.com): The Red Onions bring it like *Fun House*-era Stooges, with undulating bass lines and fucked up funk drumming. There's a lot of Motown wah-pedal guitar thrown in the mix over Iggy-like vocal deliveries.

The Alleged Gunmen (www.kapowrecords.com/ allegedgunmen/): The Alleged Gunmen always get the fuzzy end of the lollypop. And while the band's not dead like Marilyn, it was for a little while. The Gunmen always get the Clash comparison, which sells the band supremely short (apparently, if you have an affinity for Americana music, pop and punk, you're the Clash).. They have the best song ("New Bo Diddley") on *Let's Get Rid of LA* and a full-length for Kapow.

The Geisha Girls (www.geishamovement.com): The Geisha Girls is a really unique band ...I think that's called originality and that's certainly what the Geisha Girls sound like: an original band or: the Geisha Girls.

The Orphans (www.theorphans.net): The Orphans is the most rock n roll punk band in California since the Joneses. Alcohol, drugs, etc. these guys and gal are on it. The band's known for its incendiary live shows; where vocalist Jenny Orphan breaks whatever the venue was foolish enough to leave in her path. Not to be outdone, bassist Wade typically goes home with a broken guitar and/or bones. The Orphans play '78 style beach punk better than beach punk bands played it in '78. It's true. Imagine a band just aping an old style. You get the Sham 69's of this world and that's as pleasurable as a case of gonorrhea. The Orphans is different: the band brings it better than it's been brought before (in street terms: they come correct). Check the band's 7" out on TKO Records (www.tkorecords.com) entitled *Electric S.*

RECORD STORES

Amoeba Records (6400 Sunset Blvd., Hollywood , 323-245-6400, www.amoebamusic.com) owns Los Angeles. Opening up another record store in this area would be financial suicide. A testament to this was Aron's records — formerly the most revered record store in Los Angeles — going out of business recently. And while Amoeba is a juggernaut, it's kind of a benevolent one: the store is independently owned and donates cash to charities. The store itself is okay; and while there's a lot of good stuff at Amoeba (everything from the Velvets' studio albums to Johnny "Guitar" Watson's solo records), you're going to be hard-pressed to find the really rare, audiophile stuff (those harder to find Velvets bootlegs and Johnny "Guitar" Watson with Larry Williams records on the Okeh label, for example). Aron's Records was a better place for those esoteric albums but, sadly, it's gone the way of the dinosaur. Nevertheless, Amoeba is now the most formidable record store in Los Angeles, even taking into consideration the Home-Depot-meets-fashion-catwalk-disaster atmosphere of the store. (www.amoebamusic.com)

CD Trader (18928 Ventura Blvd., Tarzana) is in the Valley, but seeing how Amoeba devastated other record stores in LA like an atomic bomb, it deserves recognition. CD Trader is a great mid-sized store that (unlike Amoeba) has a warm mom-and-pop feel to it. And while the stock at CD Trader may be one-tenth that of Amoeba's, the quality stands shoulder-to-shoulder with anything Amoeba's packing (e.g., I picked up a 1967 Captain Beefheart original pressing on the Buddha label at CD Trader a month ago.

Headline Records (7706 Melrose Ave., www.headline records.com) is a great punk rock record store, owned by this really affable, amiable French guy (dude reminds me of Claude Bessy). If you want '60s or '70s punk, go here. Headline also has one of a kind band T-shirts: everything from the Clash to Radio Birdman. The store holds shows from time to time, so make sure you check its website periodically. Headline is open noon to 8 p.m. everyday.

AND BUY THIS RECORD

Let's Get Rid of LA: 2002's *Let's Get Rid of LA* was to Los Angeles what that late '70s no wave collection was to New York. Put together by the magnificent Sondra Albert (writer), Kat Jetson (journalist, owner of Project Infinity Records, www.projectinfinityrecords.com), Gabriel Hart, and Chris Ziegler (journalist), *Let's Get Rid of LA* introduced sixteen vibrant LA punk bands to a slew of benighted listeners. A couple of the groups (the Pinkz, Neon King Kong) broke up before the compilation came out, and in the four years since its release, several more have imploded. Regardless, this collection caught lightning in a bottle, with many of the bands from the comp still going strong today. Good luck finding it; this bad boy's been out-of-print for a while, but well worth the search. A big round of applause is due to the two guys and two gals who really worked hard to make this happen. Thanks a lot!

ZINES

It's sad, but I can only recommend **Razorcake** (www.razorcake.com)as a zine based outta LA. Todd Taylor runs it and he's aces. If a band matters in LA, Razorcake has covered them.

SNACKS

The **Del Taco** on Santa Monica Boulevard in Hollywood is the best place to pick up Americanized Mexican food at 3 a.m., after a show or whatever. I've never entered this place with a blood alcohol level under .12. Even drunk, I can still find it: it's off Highland, impossible to miss. The great thing about this particular Del Taco is the cast of characters which assemble there; one time I was completely drunk after a show and these two gay guys started fighting. They fought with diatribes aimed at each other's garb: "Nice shoes, honey. Where'd you get 'em? Ross?"

It was hilarious; I could never make up generalities this banal. Aspiring pimps also hang out here. And in case you're in the need, there's a donut store across the street where you can pickup a glazed twist, a large coffee and a tranny for twenty bucks. (Editors' note: Not to mention an eightball of meth.) This Del Taco is LA's answer to the diner in *Last Exit To Brooklyn* .

Astro Burger (5601 Melrose Ave., Hollywood, 323-469-1924) is good, but not as good as the Del Taco (I can talk to trannies there). If we're talking about food, then yeah, Astro Burger is way better. The place has a large vegetarian menu as well as real meat stuff. Again, no trannies hang here, but the food is pretty sublime. (Maybe buy food here and take it to the Del Taco on Highland.) Make sure you bring cash, though: Astro Burger doesn't accept debit or credit cards.

The Brite Spot (1918 W. Sunset Blvd, Echo Park, 213-484-9800) is a place that gets trashed by hipsters, yet they all seem to congregate there. Some of the complaints I've heard are: A) it's too expensive, and B) that the people who work there are elitist hipsters. Well, A maybe semi-true, but B is not (one lady who works there is seventy-something, way too old for hipster status). (Editors' note: We think she's pretty hip and aspire to be like her in the distant, *very* distant future.) Anyway, I'm sick of using the word "hipster." And, yes, some of the people who work there may be semi-crotchety, but so are the burned out ladies and alcoholic ex-cons working your local Denny's (working food fucking sucks; be glad you don't). The Brite Spot's a nice place with fantastic food (a lot of vegetarian choices). It's located right next to **the Echo**, and a great place to eat before or after a show (it's open till 4 a.m.). Fuck what you may have heard and eat there.

King Taco (2020 W. Pico Blvd., LA, 213-384-8115) is great because it's cheap, low-grade, really *good* Mexican food. You'll get fat eating here, which maybe a no-go for you guys in girl's pants.

The Alcove Cafe (1929 Hillhurst Ave., Los Feliz, 323-644-0100) is this ritzy place on Hillhurst. I ate here once with my sister and her nice boyfriend (he makes a lot more money than I do). I'm broke, so this place was a one-time deal. It had great food. If you have money, go here. They have really good hummus and cakes. Also, a lot of people in this area do cocaine. When you inhale that magical powder, you tend not to eat. Some couple next to me was clearly on the drug and left a huge plate of untouched food. I went into George Orwell *Down and Out in London and Paris* mode and thought about grabbing their untouched fries. Out of respect for my sister (I didn't want to embarrass her), I 86'ed the idea. REMINDER: This is a good place to scavenge for food.

BARS

The Short Stop (1455 Sunset Blvd., Silver Lake, 213-482-4942) is the only bar I sometimes go to. I seldom go to bars cause I never have the money, plus I'd rather just get drunk at home and listen to Gene Clark and Gun Club records. Anyway, that's me. If I have the money, I go here. The Short Stop's is great for two reasons: The juke box is loaded with MC5, the Riverboat Gamblers and the Velvet Underground; and Alexis and Namella. These two (along with Jenny Orphan from the Orphans and a girl named Ginger) have a thing called **Girl Skool**, which is really a name for their "DJ crew". ANYWAY, I don't think they ever do it here, but Alexis practically lives here and she's one of my favorite people to see drunk.

The Bigfoot Lodge (3172 Los Feliz Blvd., Los Feliz, 323-662-9227) is pretty cool. Alexis and Nmrella also do Girl Skool here. The place has a projector and sometimes they play old punk documentaries. Drinks are not too expensive, which sometimes breaks my drinking alone streaks. The atmosphere is nice and, as the name implies, rustic.

LA VIDA LOCA DE LA LINA
Lina Lecaro

Like the gal with the closet full of clothes and nothing to wear (okay, that's me), it can be hard for LA night hoppers to choose where to booze and schmooze sometimes. There is so goddamn much to do here that sometimes, nothing feels like it *will* do. The house party in Echo Park, the raging Tinseltown dance club, or that ultra-hyped band on the Sunset Strip? Chose the wrong one and you might be kicking yourself tomorrow when your pals call to tell ya about the fab time they had at the thing you didn't go to. But there are ways to increase the odds when you're looking for a good time in the motley Mecca that is La La Land. It's just about what you're in the mood for. Here, a lil' roundup of after-dark alternatives to suit your tastes whether you're looking to bang your booty, your head or, uh, something else.

HIPSTERWOOD VS. HIPSTERLAKE

Though "Hipster" is officially a dirty word these days, that hasn't stopped a certain contingent of kiddies with cool haircuts and disheveled garb from being crowned LA's reigning hip kids. Get these scrawny, vintage-clad nymphs to your club/bar and the rest of the shaggy wannabes will follow. But which is the hippest hood in LA when it comes to nightlife? Check out some of Hollywood and Silver Lake's hippest hubs, and decide for yourself.

HOLLYWOOD
Drinkin'

The **Three Clubs**' (1123 N. Vine St., Hollywood, 323-462-6441) cool factor has ebbed and flowed over the years, but it's dark, not quite swank/not quite dive vibe continues to pack 'em in. DJs play everything from rock during the week to dance music on weekends. Avoid the warriors and hang with the regulars, Mon-Thurs. Further down on Vine, it's the appropriately named **Vine** (1235 N. Vine St., Hollywood, 323-960-0800), a black and red-lacquered space that's definitely sizzling as of late, with rockin' Thursdays courtesy of those very bad **Buddyhead.com** boys and the guest-list-only indie-fest known as **Pash** on Fridays. If you're not on the list, come early, or don't come at all. Perhaps the most flamboyant mini-mall bar anywhere, **Lava Lounge** (1533 N. La Brea Ave., Hollywood, 323-876-6612, www.lavahollywood.com) rocks with a faux lava-rock fountain and weird lounge acts and live bands.

Dancin'

It's a jailbait playground at **Moscow** at **Boardners** (1652 N. Cherokee Ave., Hollywood, 323-769-5001, boardners.com) with new wave-style bands and DJs spinning indie. (Boardners other popular night, **Bar Sinister** on Saturdays attracts a decidedly older, more dramatically-dressed group: there's an all black/goth dress code.) **The Ruby** (7070 Hollywood Blvd., Hollywood, 323-467-7070) also shines for indie-rock and retro-obsessed twenty-somethings, with goth and industrial night **Perversion** on Thursdays, '80s shindig **Beat It** on Sundays and rock rave **Bang** on Saturdays.

Rockin'

The crème de la crème of hip havens has gotta be **Cinespace** (6356 Hollywood Blvd., Hollywood, 323-817-3456, www.cine-space.com) and its Tuesday events, where nearly every buzz band of the moment (Bloc Party, Kaiser Chiefs) has taken the stage and punky-looking types dance to ironically bad hip hop and '80s schlock in the front room.

SILVER LAKE
Drinkin'

The dimly lit **4100 Bar** (4100 Sunset Blvd., Silver Lake, 323-666-4460) continues to attract the Eastside art tart set, as does the Chinese-themed **Good Luck Bar** (1514 Hillhurst Ave., Los Feliz, 323-666-3524) where anyone from 9 to 5ers to slacker types (not to mention movie lovers: the **Vista theatre** is right next door) actually can get lucky sometimes. I've seen it. A more tatted lot flock to **Bigfoot Lodge** (3172 Los Feliz Blvd., Los Feliz, 323-662-9227) for its kitschy log cabin feel (complete with Smokey the Bear statue). We heart BF's punk rock karaoke on Mondays. Swingers of all stripes still have love for the **Dresden Room** (1760 N. Vermont Ave., Los Feliz, 323-665-4294) where lounge lovahs Marty and Elayne are still "Staying Alive" and "Livin' La Vida Loca" (my song!) nightly. An even nuttier old hut, and I do mean hut, **Tiki Ti** (4427 W. Sunset Blvd., Silver Lake, 323-669-9381, www.tiki-ti.com) continues to be beloved by cocktail crazies. Just be cautious of their deceptively sweet, ass kickin' drinks or you might be deserted on this tiny isle for a while. TT's been getting a run for money lately, now that Seattle's **Cha Cha Lounge** (2375 Glendale Blvd., Silver Lake, 323-660-7595) has come to the area. The super-kitschy spot meshes island-style chotchkees with Mexican touches: the tabletops feature portraits of Latin trannies.

Dancin'

Akbar (4356 Sunset Blvd., Silver Lake, 323-665-6810) started off as gay/mixed bar and now it's a full-fledged dance-o-rama with DJs spinning dance hits, old school and booty grinds. And honey, they do grind here. Similarly, former cop bar **The Short Stop** (1455 Sunset Blvd., Echo Park, 213-482-4942) has evolved into a dance space over the years with great spinsters (DJ Pubes, DJ Me, DJ You) pumpin' up the volume in its red-hued dance room. One of my fave (free) places to boogie in any hood.

Rockin'

Mainstream media has caught on to Silver Lake's burgeoning music scene, and while that might mean the inevitable demise of most rock contingents, it hasn't affected **Spaceland** (1717 Silver Lake Blvd., Silver Lake, 323-661-4380, www.clubspaceland.com), the epicenter of musical activity in S'Lake. Quite the opposite, this club continues to get the best new buzz bands from LA and beyond. Starving artists (local and otherwise) continue to haunt Mondays, which are always free and feature residencies from the indie fave du jour. The Spaceland camp also runs **The Echo** (1822 Sunset Blvd., Echo Park, 213-413-8200, www.attheecho.com) which features sounds ranging from punk to electroclash to reggae and dub, not to mention groovy dance nights like queeny crush Dragstrip 66, mashup party Bootie LA and indie/brit pop bop Hang the DJs. Equally unglossed but just as gregarious atmosphere-wise, the **Silver Lake Lounge** (2906 Sunset Blvd., Silver Lake, 323-666-2407, www.foldsilverlake.com) is the spot for boho hobo types. Low covers, cheap libations and gritty bands that aren't afraid to turn up the decibel level in such a small room. Bring earplugs.

THE CAHUENGA CLUSTERFUCK

More Hollywood hi-jinx (some hip, some haughty — as in Paris Hilton "that's hot" haughty) can be found all on one street. Hey, at least you only have to pay for parking once, and with the greedy lot gougers in this area, that's something!

Drinkin'

The Beauty Bar (1638 Cahuenga Blvd, Hollywood, 323-464-7676, www.beautybar.com) offers manicures and martinis, but that gimmick ain't what keeps this rockin,' parlor-style place sitting pretty. It's the crowd, a mix of inked-up band dudes and their groupies and Cahuenga stompers looking to avoid the bridge and tunnel babes on nearby Hollywood Blvd. An even punkier alternative, the dark and tiny **Burgundy Room** (1621-1/2 N. Cahuenga Blvd., Hollywood, 323-465-7530) is a good place to be drunk and be discreet. It's really dim in there. **Star Shoes** (6364 Hollywood Blvd., Hollywood, 323-462-7827, www.starshoes.org) may be around the corner but it's part of the Cahuenga chaos too, as most hop and back and forth between it and Beauty. The covetable shoes on display add to its charm, at least for us ladies.

Dancin'

Most of Cahuenga's dance clubs have gone from hot to not, but that just means that regular folk can actually get in now. So, if you wanna hang with regular folk (i.e., mallrats and jocks) go to the following: **Concorde** (1835 N. Cahuenga Blvd., Hollywood, 323-464-5662, www.concordela.com) once the site of bashes for Ben Affleck and Jessica Simpson, offers hip-hop, '80s and Top 40 for a multi-culti crowd. **White Lotus** (1743 N. Cahuenga Blvd., Hollywood, 323-463-0060, www.whitelotushollywood.com) is a restaurant and nightclub attracting scantily clad sake and sushi lovers, not to mention dance floor whores. Speaking of which, **XES** (1716 N. Cahuenga Blvd., Hollywood, 323-461-8190), "sex" spelled backwards, is anything but subtle about its vibe. Stripper poles, red and black décor, and sexy sounds make for the 'huenga's trashiest grind time.

DOWNTOWN DECADENCE

Downtown ain't just about designer knock-offs or scoring smack anymore. It's becoming a nightlife destination, too. Though you might still have to pay a bum to "watch" your car now and again, it's almost worth it.

Drinkin'

The rooftop bar at the **Standard Downtown** (550 S. Flower St, Downtown, 213-892-8080, www.standard hotel.com) has an awesome view of the city, a heated swimming pool (skinny-dipping has been known to happen, especially after a couple of apple martinis), and private, pod-like waterbed tents for canoodling. Dig the décor at the **Golden Gopher** (417 W. 8th St., Downtown, 213-623-9044, golden gopherbar.com), an old space that's enjoyed new life since bar king Cedd Moses took over and added opulent yet campy touches like art deco columns and golden gopher-shaped lamps. There's even a small liquor store inside the place. Moses also runs **The Broadway Bar** (830 South Broadway, Downtown, 213-614-9909, thebroadwaybar.net), next to the Orpheum theatre, a groovy two-level space featuring a bitchin' jukebox ('70s porn music, Sinatra, and current indie faves) and hunky bartenders.

VELVET ROPE-BURNERS

Got 20 bucks for valet parking? $300 for a bottle service table? Famous friends? The patience of a saint? Then you might get into the places below.

Drinkin'

It doesn't attract the star power it used to, but there's still a stellar beauty to the **Skybar** (8440 SunsetBlvd., West Hollywood, 323-650-8999), especially on a clear night. The poolside hang at the Hotel Mondrian offers great views and of course, other kinds of heavenly bodies (lots o' models and the modelizers who covet them). The Sunset Strip **Standard** Hotel bar (8300 Sunset Blvd., West Hollywood, 323-650-9090) is also less of a scene than it used to be, but the slick retro feel remains popular with local biz wigs. For a place co-owned by rockers (Tommy Lee and Dave Navarro), **Rokbar** (1710 N. Las Palmas Ave., 323-461-5600, www.rokbaronline.com) is actually pretty un-rockin'. It's too Hard Rock café-like inside, but at least the music — AC/DC, The Stones, etc. — has some edge. Still the best of the upscale drinkin' spots in my book, **Bar Marmont** (8171 Sunset Blvd., West Hollywood, 323-650-0575, www.chateaumarmont.com), with its vintage look and tasty grub, is always a treat. If you're into the celeb-oggling, you might be rewarded here, but the odds are increased tenfold at the adjoining Chateau Marmont, where famous types are often caught by fiendish photogs after their overnight trysts.

Dancin'

The crowds at **Basque** (1707 North Vine St, Hollywood, 323-464-1654, basquehollywood.com) range from sexy to scary depending on the promotion but the staff are definitely the former: hot bartender gals wear fetishy corset ensembles and the go-go dancers gyrate behind glass windows. A more Miami-style mix can be seen at **The Cabana Club** (1439 N. Ivar Ave., Hollywood, 323-463-0005, www.cabanaclub hollywood.com), adjacent to pricey meat and greet Sterling Steakhouse. Cozy cabanas and DJs spinning everything from lounge to techno to rock attracts B-listers and their entourages in droves. A cool hang during summer, I hate on the place when its cruisers make for too much traffic around the nearby Arclight theatres or Amoeba Music. There's no air traffic at **LAX** (1714 Las Palmas Ave., Hollywood, 323-464-0171, www.laxhollywood.com) but it does get packed on the tiny dance floor, especially when DJ AM (Nicole Richie's on again/off again squeeze and a part owner) spins his wild mash-ups of rock and hip hop. DJ Samantha Ronson (Mick's daughter) spins similarly disparate mixes at the star-packed Wednesday party at **Mood** (6623 Hollywood Blvd, Hollywood, 323- 464-6663, www.moodla.com). Don't even try to get into this one unless you're a famous dude or a hot chick. Ditto Saturdays. Over at **Privilege** (8117 Sunset Blvd., Hollywood, 323-654-0030, www.sbeent.com), which old-timers might remember was once the purple-plastered metal house The Coconut Teaser, the door is just as tough, especially on Saturdays when uberpromoter Brent Bolthouse welcomes Hollywood's most infamous tabloid tarts. I've almost hit a paparazzi with my car

getting out of the parking lot here on more than one occasion...
and I ain't sorry.

EAT TO THE BEAT

Who doesn't like to see and hear great music while they're
a-munchin'?

Flamenco dinner shows are just part of the tastiness you'll
find at **El Cid** (4212 Sunset Blvd., Silver Lake, 323-668-0318,
www.elcidla.com). The place has also got an array of dance
and live band nights, and a good-for-hangovers brunch on
weekends featuring feisty senior jazzster Gerrie Thill on drums.
With its loud rock and roll soundtrack, yummy comfort food
and glam-themed drinks (there's even one named after Rodney
Bingenheimer!), **Jones** (7205 Santa Monica Blvd., West
Hollywood, 323-850-1727) remains a fun place to chow and
chatter. No chattering over at **Largo** (432 N. Fairfax Ave.,
Hollywood, 323-852-1073, www.largo-la.com) though,
especially during musician-producer Jon Brion's celebrated
eve of music on Fridays. The food ain't too shabby either. For
a rowdier crowd (Lemmy Killmeister's still a regular) and
greasier grub (the pizza rules) go to the **Rainbow Bar & Grill**,
(9015 Sunset Blvd., West Hollywood, 310-278-4232,
rainbowbarandgrill.com) which is full of local (long-haired)
color. Down the street, check out **The Key Club** (9039 Sunset
Blvd., West Hollywood, 310-274-5800, www.keyclub.com),
a multi-tiered space featuring current artists of all genres (some
on national tours, others local wannabes) and an excellent
restaurant on its top floor. And if you're in the mood for raw,
as in music and fish, belly up to **Zen** (2609 Hyperion Ave.,
Silver Lake, 323-665-2929) where sushi and indie rock go
hand in hand.

OH SO ALIVE

So many places to rawk, so little time.

Though it's most popular these days as an electronic dance music venue, **Avalon** (1735 N. Vine St., Hollywood, 323-462-3000, avalon hollywood.com) — formerly The Palace — still offers some of the best touring acts around during the early evening. The sounds are louder and go later at the **Dragonfly** (6510 Santa Monica Blvd., Hollywood, 323-466-6111, www.dragonfly.com) which showcases a mix of live rock and rock hybrids seven nights a week, though nothing rages as hard as Taime Downe's old Pretty Ugly Club. **The Joint** (8771 W. Pico Blvd., West LA, 310-275-2619) usually showcases so-so rockers nightly, but it's worth noting for its "Big Monday" night jams, featuring guitar hero Waddy Wachtel and his rockstar friends. I saw and met friggin' Keith Richards here! In the space formerly known as the Garage, the **Little Temple** (4159 Santa Monica Blvd., Santa Monica, 323-660-4550, musaics.com/littletemple) offers a nice selection of DJs and soulful live acts, adding a whole never flava to the area. A more off the beaten path pit, **Mr. T's Bowl** (5261-1/2 N. Figueroa Ave., Highland Park, 323-256-7561) still bowls me over with its kooky performers and lineups. Even more low key — though not low volume — **The Smell** (247 S. Main St., Downtown, thesmell.org) has choice underground sounds and an all-ages crowd. Like its little sis mentioned above, **Temple Bar** (1026 Wilshire Blvd., Santa Monica, 310-393-6611, www.templebarlive.com) books rhythmic acts ranging from hip-hop to funk bands, and impromptu jam sessions often pop up, too. Though Johnny Depp bought out of the **Viper Room** (8852 Sunset Blvd., West Hollywood, 310-358-1880, www.viperroom.com), the place still has a solid mix of rock nightly, and even the occasional rockstar sighting (Prince did some unannounced sets here recently), but watch out for overzealous security! Down the strip, **The Roxy** (9009 Sunset Blvd., West Hollywood, 310-276-2222, www.theroxyon sunset.com) continues to book some great shows, as does **The Troubadour** (9081 Santa Monica Blvd., West Hollywood, 310-276-6168, www.troubadour.com) but sadly, the **Whisky-A-Go-Go** (8901 Sunset Blvd. West Hollywood, 310-652-4202, www.whiskyagogo.com) has gone from a legendary music hub to a pay-to-play haven for bad metal bands from the Valley.

Whew, think I need a disco nap now...

FETISH L.A.
Jayson Marston

Okay, so you want to be a kinky freakazoid in LA? Here's where to start... but remember, this isn't the be-all, end-all guide to perversion in Hollywood, just a jumping- off point.

You will want to go shopping for some gear at **665** (8722 Santa Monica Blvd; W. Hollywood, 323-854-7276, www.665leather.com) and **Mr. S** (4232 Melrose Ave., LA, www.mr-s-leather.com) are two shops that sell only high quality toys and clothing. If you want to clamp it, catheterize it or simply chastise it these shops will have what you need. Both stock standard leather and fetish gear, and also offer some of their own creations. 665 recently expanded to 2,000 square feet, which houses their assortment of bondage/ dungeon furniture. Both shops make and stock items for all genders. People who know kink and kinky fashion well staff both shops. Don't be shy, they are all experienced players and nothing can make them blush! If you are visiting LA, be sure to check out their websites beforehand and make a list of what you want, otherwise you'll be the proverbial kid in a candy store... even though the kid in the candy store probably wasn't being helped by a guy in a pair of leather chaps...

If you have a burning desire to be a porn star or simply have a burning sensation during urination, head to **AIM HealthCare Foundation** (14241 Ventura Blvd Sherman Oaks; 818-981-5681, www.aim-med.org). AIM is where denizens of the adult film industry go to get their STD testing and treatment done. They offer HIV/STD testing and treatment as well as counseling for sexual health. AIM offers an early detection HIV test and the staff is extremely knowledgeable. The services offered are available for the open-minded general public as well.

If getting pierced is something you desire, I recommend **Thirteen B.C.** (7661 Melrose Ave., LA, www.thirteenbc.com). A safe, clean shop, the staff is very well-trained and has lots of experience making holes. Owner Taj Waggaman has pierced many people including celebrities from porn to mainstream movies stars. If you want to get tattooed, try **Melrose Tattoo** (7661 Melrose Ave., LA, 323-655-4345) Dean Berton and Joey Galigher do really great work out of this shop. **Incognito Tattoo** (750 East Colorado St., Pasadena, 626-584-9448, www.incognitotattoo.com) is a great shop where Jason Schroeder does some great work also. These shops are staffed by well-trained people, which mean you may not get the Hollywood Boulevard flash-off-the-wall prices but you *will* get quality work done. FYI: it is appropriate to tip either your piercer or tattoo artist, and haggling over prices is *not* appropriate — hey, these people aren't fishmongers!

So now you are dressed and ready for action. If you are looking for man-to-man action, **The Slammer** (3688 Beverly

Blvd., LA, 323-388-8040, www.slammerclub.com) is a good place to find it. It's 2,000 feet of legal and creative erotic space. Slammer also offers HIV and STD testing on site. Any true sex pig worth his chaps in gold will be here the first night in town and every night thereafter. As far as nightclubs and theme nights, they come and go so fast that by the time you read this, they may be done and over. **Tattoo Chris** is one promoter that has great parties for men. He has the ability to get 600 of some of the hottest guys in LA to the Valley. This may not sound like much but try getting 10 guys to meet you in the Valley and see how it goes. He always has plenty of things going on, so check it out at www.tattoochris.com.

For a more hetero slant, there are many different parties that go on monthly. **Courtney Cruz** is one of the most beautiful women in the Los Angeles fetish scene. She is often part of many events and a Los Angeles treasure. Her site, www.courtneycruz.com, will let you know what she's up to. For the ladies into other ladies, check out Wednesdays at the **Eagle LA** (4219 Santa Monica Blvd., Silver Lake, 323-669-9472, www.eaglela.com). Miss Kim is the first lady bartender at this bar, she has the sweetest smile. The Eagle LA has recently opened and has started with a great crowd of men. It has more of a leather and bear crowd but all are welcome.

There are many great bars that host monthly and weekly parties. **MJ'S** (2810 Hyperion, Silver Lake, 323-660-1503, www.mjsbar.com) is a great place with a variety of nights. One place to go looking for current fetish events is **www.fetishdomain.com**. This site lists practically everything and will pretty much dial you into the LA fetish scene. The **LA Weekly** also has club listings, events listings, and personal ads, and all the stores I have listed will have flyers for different clubs, special events, and play parties. Remember: be friendly, it gets you laid.

WHERE THE BOYS ARE
Deadlee

The Dingoes are ready to fight, freak, or fuck their way back to Montebello. These gay gangsters, like The Warriors of the famed '70s movie, are on the run back to their home turf, can you diiig iit?! Standing in their path are some of the raunchiest, nastiest, out-for-cum gay boys in Los Angeles. It will take every bit of their DL street skillz and over-seven-inch weapons to make it back alive. Like the Lady DJ who tracked the Warriors' whereabouts, I will be your MC spittin' knowledge of LA underground to where, clang clang clang (bottles rattling), gay boys come out to plaaaaay!

DOWNTOWN

Our Dingoes are walking down a street lined with taxicabs having just been released from the **Twin Towers** (LA County Jail, 411 Bauchet St., 213-473-6100). Gay boys in jail are labeled K-11s and are housed in units 51-53. If it's bad boys you desire, get arrested and pass the test to get admitted to the gay side of County Jail. You may want to brush up on your gay history like when the Stonewall rebellion started or the names of some gay magazines. Once inside, you will be in a the gay Thunder Dome where boys always make the best of a bad situation. There will be hot fashion shows with the latest in ripped sheets, and even gay weddings. It's well-known that on the queer side when the lights go down, the tents come up. There are plenty of signs posted that sex in jail is illegal... but condoms are passed out. You may want to double up since a lot of the boys are repeat offenders, hustlers, and drug users. After you are released, like our Dingoes, you'll see there are plenty of parked cars on Bauchet St. *eager* to give a freed jailbird a ride and possibly a place to stay.

The Dingoes need a cold beer and the best place is the cantina **Jalisco Inn** (245 S. Main Street, 213-680-0658) located on the edge of Skid Row, you will be jettisoned to Mexico upon entry. An old jukebox plays 45s of Paquita del Barrio while sexy bar *mamis* stuff limes down the head of the coldest Coronas. The clientele is a mix of new Latino immigrants, Chicanos, and punk boys who have wandered over from **The Smell** (247 S. Main Street, www.thesmell.org, enter through alley). Pink boys with a little stink take in the best in underground, punk and rock acts at this art gallery/performance space. So jump around like a 14-year-old girl and munch on vegan goodies. No alcohol served!

The Dingoes need to clean off the stench so they head to **Midtowne Spa** (615 Kohler St. 213-680-1838, www.mid townespa.com) for five floors of fun. The sundeck and the basement maze are my favorite amenities, but I will never forget my first fisting experience in one of their private rooms. The Dingoes have busted plenty of nuts and must get out of

Downtown, hey what better way than the **Los Angeles Metro System** aka MTA (www.mta.net). Pick a color, ORANGE, RED, GREEN, BLUE, and ride all day for just three bucks. I have had my share of glances, quick feels and the occasional stray follow me home after a ride on our public transit. I am MC DEADLEE and our Dingoes have just been spotted coming up from the subway on Beverly and Vermont!

RAMPART / ECHO PARK / SILVER LAKE

The Rampart District is known for its crooked cops, and is also home to the best gloryhole cocks. **The Slammer** (3688 Beverly Blvd., 213-388-8040, www.slammerclub.com) features hand-crafted slings, water sports, and a new patio. It's LA's best sex club. This place will turn a top into a nasty bottom. I was once bent over for an Asian, an Armenian, a Latino, and a black guy... in that order! **Echo Park** (between Echo Park Blvd and Glendale) is home to Mousie and Sad Girl, from *Mi Vida Loca*; down low cholos and gay yuppies cruise after dark. So if your down for your shit, meet at the logs, and don't be a *leva*! Cops do make occasional sweeps so be on the lookout! Our Dingoes have worked up an appetite and dine at **Rodeo Mexican Grill** (1721 W. Sunset Blvd., 213-953-1010). This is the Latino version of West Hollywood where brown boys and their familia, friends and lovers eat good cheap food. The *camarones* and *carne asada* plates are highly recommended.

The Dingoes cruise in their '63 Impalas down Glendale into Silver Lake for a rimjob and I'm not talking about the car. Every Tuesday **MJ'S** (2810 Hyperion, 323-660-1503, www.mjsbar.com) reeks of testosterone in LA's sexiest club night. Strippers and freak boys grind their gears to funk, rock, and hip hop. When the DJ played Chicano Rap God Lil' Rob and filled the floor with hot *pelones*, I knew this club was *firme*! **The Other Side** (2538 Hyperion Ave., 323-661-0618, www.flyingleapcafe.com) would bring out the homo in any thug for a night of cabaret at one of LA's best kept secrets. So sit next to a hot grandaddy and have a "Liza with a Z" kind of night at the gay piano bar. (Editors' note: Once, when we inquired as to who was tinkling the ivories that week, the bartender said proudly, "He used to be the *second* Construction Worker in the Village People!")

Hey boppers, our Dingoes have marked their territory and continue down Hyperion to **Akbar** (4356 W. Sunset Blvd., 323-665-6810). On the first Sunday of the month it is **Break-a-way**, where Rudy Bleu of Scutterfest and La Polla Loca fame has all the boys in their tighty whities and jockstraps "fucking the pain away" with guest DJs like Peaches!

If leather is your pleasure, the old **Gauntlet II** is now called **Eagle LA** (4291 Santa Monica Blvd., 323-669-9472, www.eaglela.com). In the tradition of all Eagle clubs, they keep it rough 'n' stuff in their chaps and cuffs!

HOLLYWOOD

The jukebox plays the Christina Aguilera version of "Lady Marmalade," while chicks with dicks stand on the table and do a "Gichie gichie ya ya dada Mocha Chocalata ya ya" for their admirers. You have just entered the **Blacklite** (1159 N. Western Ave., 323-469-0211) (Editors' note: We call it the "Black Out") but I prefer the original by LaBelle, and that will just be one of the showstoppers that you will witness at **The Study** (1723 N. Western Ave., 213-464-9221). (Editors' note: There was a time when the neon sign was broken and the only letters lit up said, "HE STUD.") Mz. Laverne is host of the best drag show every Friday night in the new and improved club. Adios Mutha Fucka is the dranky drank of the night and these girls give you Patty ready to soar or Whitney looking for crack on the floor, *allegedly*. Sunday brings out all the Homo Thugs who cruise over after a day parked in the loop of **Griffith Park**.

The Dingoes head south of the border to **Tempo** (5520 Santa Monica Blvd., 323-466-1094, www.clubtempo.com). This Latino club has Coronas *grandes toda la noche cada Jueves* and *Mariachi y banda los Domingos*. VIVA LA RAZA! If you have had a few too many cervezas, cross the street to the taco truck **El Matador** (1174 N. Western Ave., after 7 p.m.) Hungry *paisas* munch on the best *chorizo, cabeza, tripas,* and *al pastor* tacos. These boys have appetites and will be willing to try *your* carne next. The Dingoes feel the rushes coming from the "hustling bar" on Selma Avenue made infamous in John Rechy's novel, *The Sexual Outlaw*, **The Spotlight** (1601 Cahuenga Blvd., 323-467-2425, spotlightbar.com) host to the club with the same name every Thursday, Sexual Outlaws — Bruce LaBruce, James St. James, and John Waters are just some of the gay rebels who have graced this space.

Our underage Dingoes have been spotted sucking the milk from the big breasts of Miss Delicious, who hosts the 18 and over club Delicious at **Arena** (6655 Santa Monica Blvd., 323-462-1291). After a night of hard dancing, the Dingoes need to get clean. The Gay and Lesbian Center's Youth Drop-In, **Jeff Griffith Youth Center** (7051 Santa Monica Blvd., 323-993-7501, www.lagaycenter.org) offers meals, showers, laundry, clothing, GED prep, and the Internet!

INTERNET

The Dingoes are about to surf the net. **www.myspace.com** is the new meeting place for friends, forget the diner. Hot music pages for your favorite bands, and personalized pages! **www.tribe.net** is raunchier and more community-based, **www.bilatinmen.com** and **www.latinboyz.com** have great message boards and hot videos! My favorite is actually **www.adam4adam.com**, you can search for your boy by the little details that matter the most. At any given time, at least a thousand boys are cruising this site in LA. So if you want a guy, 33, mix, from Echo Park, shaved head, cut, 7.5 inch penis, not into pnp, then it's just a click away!

THE VALLEY

Like oh my God, dude, the Dingoes have landed in the Valley — how gnarly! **Club L** (4923 Lankershim Blvd., 818-769-7722, www.clubl.net)**:** Where this "L word" stands for lucky, because Valley boys are easy, sleazy, and — like those housewives — very desperate. This NoHo club has a great karaoke night, and a dance floor surrounded by mirrors. Check your moves out, and watch for stray hands because you might just score before you leave the club! A lot of Valley boys don't venture over the hill so if you are looking for fresh faces, this is definitely the place. If you want to pump the gasoline and get *todo mojado papi*, dance to reggaeton at **Coco Bongo** (19655 Sherman Way, 818-998-8464, www.cocobongo.info)**.** *Travesti* shows, Coronita buckets, and $3 tequila shots all night long.

MONTHLY

There are two monthly clubs that mostly cater to African American and Latino brothas. **Boytrade** (www.boytrade.com) is every last Friday of the month, while **First Fridayz** (www.firstfridayzla.com) is every first Friday like its name. The locations change, so check the web for the 411!

Our gay gangsters the Dingoes have been banged, jacked, and sucked dry; and all this without stepping foot in West Hollywood. Who knew Los Angeles had a different side to *Queer As Folk*, steroid, tweak-filled white party boys? The

Dingoes have made it back to their home turf of Montebello and are down for one last **Cockfight**, which is every Wednesday at **Chico** (2915 W. Beverly Blvd., 323-721-3403, www.clubchico.com). Old skool gangsters and fresh-tweezed *chulos* get close in this crammed East Los bar. DJ Ernie spins rap, hip hop, and reggaeton to celebrate the Dingoes return. The best part about Los Angeles is its diversity, but the worst is its segregation. Even in our gay ghetto we tend to party with only our kind. So even if you're like Dorothy in Oz clicking her ruby slippers — "There's no place like home" — be adventurous and open-minded, and pay a visit to a gay side different from your own.

Alrato and laterz!

DUDE, YOU'RE KILLNG MY CRUISE
Lesbian L.A.
Bett Williams

A gay man once explained the rules for picking up men in San Francisco bars. Men hang around in tight pants with a drink in hand, whether it be Coke or whiskey, leaning on a wall, cruising. If you see someone from work or even a friend, it is not polite to talk to them for too long. It's also not rude for the person holding up the wall to say, "Dude, you're killing my cruise."

Lesbians repeat after me: "Dude, you're killing my cruise." Most of the LA women I know who frequent lesbian bars hardly ever pick up women in them. Hence, they don't get laid. Hence, they don't have relationships. Hence, they don't mature. There is a reason they don't get laid, don't have relationships, and don't mature: THEY GO TO LESBIAN

BARS WITH THEIR FRIENDS. They stand around in small, vicious pods of tribal exclusivity, judgment and gossip, then they complain about not meeting anybody. Talk about killing a cruise.

Number one rule, for the health and benefit of all: Try going to a lesbian bar alone, or with *one* friend, with the primary intent of not leaving unless you make out with someone in an alley or in a bathroom. I like **Here** (696 N. Robertson Blvd, West Hollywood, 310-360-8455, www.here lounge.com), a stylish bar with a dance floor and a patio, next to the always-packed **Abbey** (692 N. Robertson Blvd, West Hollywood, 310-289-8410, www.abbeyfood andbar.com), a place that's fun on Sunday afternoons when it's sunny — celebrity sightings: Chastity Bono... At Here, the dance floor gets really sweaty and sexy, especially in the area in back by the bathrooms. I hope I don't get busted by the PC police when I say that the white faces seem to disappear here, as the heat gets hotter and the word "booty" returns to one's vocabulary whether you like it or not. I like it a lot. This is another reason I like **The Palms** (8572 Santa Monica Blvd., West Hollywood, 310-652-6188, www.thepalmsbar.com) — all the hot black and Hispanic women... and Russians with accents. The other bars are ethnically diverse, but there's always an Industry dyke feel, where no matter where you come from or what race you are, you look the same as everybody else.

Okay, maybe I need to define the term "Industry dyke." Most lesbians who hang out in the bars in LA either work in the film industry or want to work in the film industry. In LA, the film industry is simply "The Industry." This has gone from a fact into a cliché, there are codes that define this particular tribe. They are basically socially conservative and despite the fact they often wear True Religion jeans and have Shane hair, they look conservative, too. Try to talk non-monogamy to them and they look at you like you are Jeffrey Dahmer, yet some come to the bar with a chick on their arm whom they refuse to introduce as their "girlfriend" because their Industry friends have advised them that it's best they appear in public as "single." If this doesn't make you sick, you are already gone — and not the right kind of gone.

The *right* kind of gone is getting drunk at the **Redhead Bar** (2218 E. First St., LA, 323-263-2995), the first lesbian bar in LA. It's so strictly Hispanic, I wondered if I was even allowed in the place without a membership card. Then, two older women, somewhere between fifty and sixty took pity on me and began to talk. They told me about getting arrested in the '50s for wearing men's clothes, how they were sent home in dresses, the humiliation of it. In moments like this I feel like being a lesbian is the most beautiful privilege because I end up in the strangest and most wonderful places full of history. I mean, if you're not going to cruise, you might as well learn something about the world, right?

The Normandy Room (8737 Santa Monica Blvd., West Hollywood, 310-659-6204) is a pool room with dirty carpet and the same people you see everywhere else, except here, they're sad, bored or trying to buy pot.

Girl Bar (Fridays, The Factory, 661 North Robertson Blvd., West Hollywood, 310-669-4551, www.girlbar.com) has a hex on it. I can't explain. Try it if you want.

I Candy (Tuesdays, 7929 Santa Monica Blvd, West Hollywood, 323-656-4000, icandylounge.com) is the newest incarnation of clubs promoted by Michelle Agnew and Linda Fusco of **Here**, **Oasis** and **The Falcon**. You will see haircuts, jeans and friendship pods as previously described.

Gauntlet II (Wednesdays, 4219 Santa Monica Blvd, LA, 323-669-9472, www.gauntletii.com) is friendship pods with piercings and more Industry dykes than even West LA. At first the gay male porn on the TV seems like a good idea, until upon researching gay male porn, you realize it's the worst, most lame, gay male porn ever. (Editors' note: It's just that the cheapskate fags at the Gauntlet II won't even invest in one chick porn flick! Consider donating.)

The Falcon (Sundays, 7213 Sunset Blvd, LA, 323-850-5350, www.falconslair.com) screens "The L Word."

Best Place to Meet Another Lesbian You Probably won't Fuck but Will be Best Friends with for at Least Six Months: The **Red Lion Tavern** (2366 Glendale Blvd., LA, 323-662-5337) This is a German-themed bar with waitresses in milkmaid outfits and a guy on a keyboard singing Neil Diamond songs and other random covers. Despite this, some angelic presence lives in the place that brings the Silver Lake community together in the best of ways.

Best Place to Bond with Straight Chicks on a Dance Floor who are Drunk and Want to Flirt and Vent about Being Sick of Gross Men (i.e., They Might Sleep with You at Least Once): **The Short Stop** (1455 Sunset Blvd., LA, 213-482-4942). This place used to be a cop bar and despite the drunk chicks, the newly sober like to rock out here on the dance floor, too. It's a nice mix but needs more of an overtly dyke presence, so get your ass over there, women.

Good If You Go Only Every Eight Months Tops: **Cheetah's** strip club (4600 Hollywood Blvd., LA, 323-660-6733, www.cheetahsofhollywood.com). Celebrity sightings: Chastity Bono.

Best Place to Pick Up Really Hot Straight or Bi Wannabe Actresses from the Midwest who Get Horny for Anyone who Gives Them Compliments: **The Cat and Fiddle** (6530 W. Sunset Blvd., Hollywood, 323-468-3800, www.catand fiddle.com). Stand by the jasmine bush that grows in the center of the fountain on a warmish March night and anyone is sexy.

HOORAY FOR HOLLYWOOD!
(AND LOS FELIZ, TOO!)

Hollywood and Los Feliz (unofficially known as East Hollywood) are full of fun, interesting things to do: tons of rock clubs, theaters, boutiques, restaurants and souvenir shops... not to mention parks, landmarks, and serendipitous diversions.

Hollywood used to be a seedy and forgotten ghost town, but for the past couple of years it has been undergoing extensive urban renewal. The area has changed more in the past two or three years than the past four or five decades, and that's *not* an exaggeration. Most Hollywood locals are ecstatic that the Movie Capital of the World has been stopped from becoming the Crack Capital of the World... Just a few years ago, it was well on its way. We also are overjoyed that the many gorgeous landmark buildings, which previously would have been razed and turned into ugly strip malls or left to crumble, are, like aging movie stars, having some "work " done. We love the fact that FINALLY people are showing interest in Hollywood itself, whether it's our contribution to pop culture or our "Dream Factory" legacy, or just the incredibly unique local flavor. We're all just dotty that Hollywood Boulevard itself is now rockin' a spiffy, clean version of its pink and black terrazzo **Walk of Fame** — and you can actually stroll the Boulevard safely, eat some decent food, see a movie, and hear live music pouring out of the many brand-spankin' new nightclubs. That's something ya couldn't have done unless you were around during the Rat Pack days — even during the late '70s, the only nightclub on the Boulevard was LA's first punk venue ever, **The Masque**, and that was in the basement of the Pussycat Theater (now a Latino Born Again church) at the corner of Hollywood and Cherokee.

So — nightlife again — and now you can also stay on the Boulevard, in the swank **Hollywood Roosevelt Hotel** (7000 Hollywood Blvd., 323-466-7000, www.hollywood roosevelt.com), which has just been fabulously re-done. It's not cheap by any means, but it is luxe and hipper than hip — their poolside club **The Tropicana** (complete with private cabanas and VIP bottle service) is in the tabloids almost weekly, because it's where Paris and Nicole, Lindsay, and the Olsens act out their poor-little-rich-girl psychodramas.

The downside of all this gentrification is that the **Kodak Theater** (and the Oscars) moved into Hollywood proper, rents have sky-rocketed, and locals almost can't afford to live here anymore, and there's never anywhere to park (even on the residential streets) unless you wanna pay twenty bucks... and then you still have to wait for a space! There are also so many tourists and suburbanites pouring into town that you have to wait in a crazy-long line for everything from the hottest new nightclubs to just getting a cuppa joe! Not that we have anything against tourists — aw, HELL no — just... Be patient, and prepared to wait. Word to the wise: if it's a club you're waiting for, most door people here really *can't* be bribed. They don't cotton to rudeness, either, so remember to be nice, okay?

Some of the refurbished Art Deco masterpieces in the 'Wood 'hood are residences, some are "destination" buildings, where you can go for a live high-end show, like the **Pantages Theater** (6233 Hollywood Blvd.) which hosts Broadway musicals, or the **Henry Fonda Music Box Theater** (6126 Hollywood Blvd., 323-856-4252, henryfonda theater.com) which hosts rock concerts, deejay nights, and the occasional dance production. They also have a beautiful rooftop patio and a great little separate bar called **The Blue Palm**. For films, visit these two fantastically revamped movie palaces: The American Cinematheque's **Egyptian Theater** (6212 Hollywood Blvd., 323-466-FILM, www.egyptiantheater.com) which shows restored classics, foreign and art films, and newer stuff, as well as hosting film festivals, Q&A sessions with famous directors, etc. The **El Capitan** (6838 Hollywood Blvd., 323-467-7674, www.elcapitantickets.com) has never looked better, and is great for kids, as they usually show Disney or Pixar films and have a live show opening every screening, a la Radio City Music Hall. If the kiddies are cranky, it's an awesome way to kill an afternoon. Also redone (and smack between both theaters) is the **Pig'n'Whistle** (6714 Hollywood Blvd., 323-463-0000, www.pignwhistle.com), which was a Raymond Chandler-era restaurant and watering hole that has been restored to its original splendor after years of being literally walled up inside a trashy pizza place. A lot of new cute stores, cafes and bars have opened, too.

Check out the strip on Hollywood Boulevard between Highland and La Brea... you'll find cute souvenir stores, coffeeshops, and a weird assortment of chainstores, like a **Hooters** practically next door to **American Apparel** (6922 Hollywood Blvd., 323-465-6312, www.americanapparel.net), an LA-based company which makes delectable fashionista T-shirts, skirts, bathing suits, and yoga pants in a plethora of colors. They have at least ten branches in Greater Los Angeles, and probably more by the time you read this. Everyone loves their stuff, it's like hipster classics, and affordable.

Anyway, across the street is **The Knitting Factory** (7021 Hollywood Blvd., 323-463-0204), a thinking person's nightclub with great food, an internet café, and two rooms featuring touring bands to underground films to spoken word and burlesque. Another good thing is that newish subway system also makes it possible to get from Hollywood to Downtown LA in about fifteen minutes. Malls, like the gigantic new one at **Hollywood and Highland** (www.hollywood andhighland.com) which houses the state-of-the-art **Kodak Theatre**, or the monstrosity that now surrounds the Pacific Theater's funky vintage **Cinerama Dome** and houses the **Arclight Theater** (Sunset and Ivar, 323-464-4226, arclightcinemas.com) are springing up like mushrooms. Everything is getting very corporate and commercial. Some of the new stuff is great - like the Arclight actually saved the Cinerama Dome which was scheduled to be razed. Try to see a movie in the Dome if you can, it's so funky and retro and... big. The Arclight also has a bar, a café with decent food, a cute bookstore, and movie stills, posters and costumes are exhibited in the lobby. Tickets are like fifteen bucks (yeah, for a movie!) but it's still kinda fun to have an usher escort you to your reserved seat to see a flick!

If you need to kill a few minutes or HOURS, just a couple steps west on Sunset from the Arclight is **Amoeba Music** (6400 Sunset, 323-246-6400, www.amoebamusic.com) Can't say enough great things about the mega-superstore of music! They have aisles and aisles of every possible kind of CD, vinyl, DVD, new and used — this place is amazing and makes other music stores obsolete... If they had a bar in there, no one would ever leave! The scene on the street outside is always interesting, too: 50-year-old Gothic bag ladies, runaway kids with rainbow mohawks and big pitbulls, hippies playing hackey-sack, 50-cent impersonators trying to chat up soccer moms, it's just bonkers.

Another new mall is the **Gateway to West Hollywood** (Santa Monica Blvd and La Brea) more 'mall-like,' it features chain restaurants such as **Daphne's Greek Café** and **Pomodoro** and also houses Hollywood **Target**, maybe the ONLY Target that has drag queens checking you into the ladies' fitting rooms... but this mall has also incorporated the landmark **Formosa Café** instead of tearing down this ancient watering hole that once hosted the likes of Lana Turner, Elvis, Marilyn Monroe, and Ava Gardner... notorious gangster Bugsy Seigal reportedly ran a numbers racket out of the back room!

More shopping: **Iguana Vintage Clothing Hollywood** (6320 Hollywood Blvd., 323-462-1010, www.iguana clothing.com) has three floors of good quality vintage threads, new and used shoes & purses, and brand new accessories like rhinestone jewelry, kooky sunglasses and wigs in every color. Even more fun is **Hollywood Toy & Costume** (6600 Hollywood, 323-464-4444, www.hollywoodtoys.com), which is the go-to store if you need to play last minute dress-up year-round. They also have every kind of wig known to mankind, as well as hats, masks, feather headdresses (both Indian and showgirl style), fairy wings, toy swords and guns, aisles and aisles of toys for kids, "collectible" toys and models, blank guns, life-sized robots, you name it.

For a fun, free day summer Sunday in Hollywood, start off with the **Hollywood Farmers Market** (open until 1 p.m. every Sunday, centered at Ivar and Selma Aves, Hollywood). Here, you can get fresh produce dirt cheap, eat excruciatingly mouth-watering tamales, and buy everything from homemade olives and freshly baked bread to vintage clothing, crafts, vitamins, jewelry and candles. While you're walking around (rare for natives!), it's still fun to amble along the **Walk of Fame** and try to find your favorite stars (everyone from Lassie to Marilyn Monroe to the Three Stooges) along the pink and black granite. Have a look to the north (towards the Hollywood Hills) and see the majestic **Capital Records Tower** (1750 N. Vine, www.hollywoodandvine.com for MP3s of new Capital releases). You probably won't see any rock stars here, but you will at **Jumbo's Clown Room** (5153 Hollywood Blvd., 323-666-1187), a hole-in-the-wall strip joint where Courtney Love used to work before Hole and Kurt. This has always been a hot spot for rock 'n' rolls types (Lemmy from Motorhead practically lives there), and features a mini-stage with pole and girls stripping to The Cramps or Prodigy.

But back to the Boulevard. If you walk west towards La Brea, you can still enjoy all the historical hand and footprints in the courtyard of **Grauman's Chinese Theatre Complex** (6925 Hollywood Blvd., 323-464-8111, www.mann theatres.com) — the front part of my platform shoes fit into Trigger's horseshoes! And they show current features for bargain prices during matinee hours. The interior of the main theater is gorgeous, all Chinois, red lacquer, coiling dragons, and oriental chandelier, and now, they even have a VIP Lounge... but the best part of Grauman's is the celebrity impersonators and characters hanging around outside, hoping to get tourists' tips as they pose for photos. You have to see this to believe it — most of these characters are so low rent, it's surprising John Waters don't hang out here on a regular basis. Imagine "Madonna" who looks like an Armenian grandmother with bleached hair; Star Wars robots with costumes made out of tinfoil... Once, on a slow, overcast day, three Spidermen got into a shoving match over "territory." You can end the day with a slightly more cultured activity: check out the schedule for the outdoor **Hollywood Bowl**'s (2301 N. Highland Ave., 323-850-2000 www.hollywood bowl.com) classical, rock, world music, and folk concerts, and occasional movie sing-alongs (*Wizard of Oz, Rocky Horror, Sound of Music*) sometimes for free or very low-cost. Pack a picnic supper and bring a blanket.

The building that *used* to house world-famous lingerie store **Frederick's of Hollywood** (6608 Hollywood Blvd.) remains a purple '20s Moderne behemoth and the interior used to be a stripper's wet dream. Alas, though Frederick's hasn't closed completely (you can find a small branch inside the mall at Hollywood and Highland), it ain't what it used to be. However, the whole south side of the Boulevard has a ton of stripper and ho-wear stores, like **Bizzy Bee** (6548 Hollywood Blvd., 323-469-4309, www.bizzybeeofhollywood.com) which is like a seductress version of a wet dream. They stock amazing colorful lingerie by Felina; Leg Avenue thigh-highs and stockings; a wall of gloves, from opera-length to metallics, fishnets, and marabou-trimmed; kinky-but-cute role-playing costumes (barely-there police outfits complete with handcuffs, microscopic Catholic school uniforms, etc.) **Playmates of Hollywood** (6438 Hollywood Blvd., 323-464-7636, www.playmatesofhollywood.com), another ooh-la-la emporium that also features costumes, boas, pasties, clubwear, cool sets of undies and rhinestone jewelry. The staff is all young and hip, and directly next door, they own **La La Shoes**, which hawks all manner of trendy footwear, from sky-high Lucite stripper pumps to Goth-chick platform boots, plus cute rocker-chick purses.

If you wanna watch gals who probably shop at Playmates takin' off their clothes, then try **Cheetah's** (4600 Hollywood Blvd., Los Feliz, 323-660-6733) which has, probably, the best and prettiest dancers working. The pole work you see here is amazing because most of the women are professional dancers in between 'regular' dance-gigs. The atmosphere is friendly, the tunes are trendy, and the drinks, though a bit pricey, are strong. A pal once remarked that Cheetah's is a great "starter" strip club: no bullshit, no hustling, just a lotta T 'n' A fun.

As far as regular bars go, there are tons, and many feature live music. A few good spots are the **Blacklite** (1159 N. Western, 323-469-0211) which used to cater mostly to transsexual prostitutes but has become a divey hipster hotspot of sorts; the **Lava Lounge** (1533 N. La Brea Ave., north of Sunset, 323-876-6612) not only makes tropical drinks loaded with fruit, parasols and plastic monkeys, but also has live entertainment. The decor is *tres exotique*, On the Boulevard itself (just west of Argyle, next to the Pantages Theater) is the **Frolic Room** (6245 Hollywood Blvd., 323-462-5890), a tiny hole-in-the-wall with a vintage Hirschfeld mural taking up one whole side, and a great jukebox. The nearby **King King** (6555 Hollywood Blvd., 323-960-9234, kingkinghollywood.com) was once a seminal '80s club which closed but re-appeared on the Boulevard. They book hot blues, Latin jazz, ska, rockabilly, and bebop as well as burlesque shows. Everyone is happy this place has made a comeback. Touring and local musicians sometimes show up to jam, such as country crooners Candye Cane and Rosie Flores, members of X and The Blasters, even legendary Cuban musicians.

Another popular bar, albeit one you can eat in — heck, the entire restaurant is a landmark — is **El Coyote** (7312

Beverly Blvd., west of La Brea, 323-939-2255, elcoyotecafe.com) which has killer margaritas, and waitresses that dress up in hoop-skirted flamenco garb and make-up that would make Divine green with envy. The decor is pure camp: velvet paintings, chandeliers shaped like bunches of grapes... some people say that the food leaves a little to be desired but the general consensus is that after one or two of the margaritas, who cares? On a macabre note, this bistro (open for the past half-century) was also the site of Sharon Tate's last meal before the Manson murders. Another cool retro Mexican joint is the **Garden of Taxco** (1113 N. Harper Ave., West Hollywood, 323-654-1746). Cool and dark, with a beamed ceiling and Mexican blankets on the tables, they don't have a menu: the waiter recites the prix fixe specials of the night. All dinners have four courses including dessert, which comes with a glass of sherry. Everything is homemade and incredible (the mole sauce is to die for).

Another exotic place to eat is **Moun of Tunis** (7445-1/2 Sunset, near Gardner, 323-874-3333, www.mounoftunis restaurant.com), a Tunisian and Moroccan restaurant, full of tented private rooms, incense, and low lights. You get your hands washed by the server, lay back on couches, and eat North African cuisine with your fingers while watching a bellydancer perform. Sharon Stone, Ethan Hawke, Johnny Depp, and the Rolling Stones are regulars here. Private rooms are available at no extra cost, call ahead to reserve. Check out the Bellydance Showcase on the third Tuesday of every month (make reservations — it always sells out) where the dinner is on special for $22. Kind of like an "open mic" for bellydancers, featuring 6-9 dancers who range in experience from students to visiting professionals. It's a rowdy fun, wiggly night.

Directly next door is **Guitar Center**, (7425 Sunset, 323-874-1060, www.guitarcenter.com) with its own little rock 'n' roll Walk of Fame where you can see the handprints of legends like Ozzy Osbourne and Alice Cooper. If you're more into gangsta rap, R&B or hip hop, you might wanna check out **Roscoe's House of Chicken and Waffles** (1518 N. Gower, north of Sunset, 323-466-7453) when bars close, or on a Sunday morning. This is more an experience than a restaurant. It's a teeny-tiny place loaded with tables, serving unbelievably fattening, amazing soul food: chicken and waffles, of course, but also greens, black-eyed peas, chitlins, etc. There's usually a line to get in and tons of limos outside. Everyone is yakking on cell-phones and checking their Palm Pilots, the women all look like Lil' Kim, Beyonce Knowles, and Mary J. Blige, and come to think of it, they're probably not clones, but the real thing!

Along these lines, there are other restaurants that serve as places to see and be seen, all of which have been around so long they're not 'flavor-of-the-month' but established, well-known pieces of Hollywood history. **Joseph's Cafe** (1775 Ivar, between Franklin and Hollywood, 323-462-8697) is THE place for "power" brunches in an unpretentious atmosphere for everyone from screenwriters to rock stars. Slurp lentil soup or lick tzatsiki off your fingers while trying not to stare at Johnny Knoxville or Marilyn Manson. They just did extensive renovations and opened a marvelous bar that's a hopping nightspot, too... read about it in *The Star*: it's a Britney & K-Fed, Paris & Stavros, kinda scene.

Over in Los Feliz is **Home** (1760 Hillhurst, 323-669-0211) which serves American food: meatloaf, burgers, breakfasts, and huge salads in a gorgeous, jungle-like garden patio. **Miceli's** (1646 Las Palmas, just south of Hollywood Blvd., 323-466-3438) and **Palermo's** (1858 N. Vermont, Los Feliz) are both age-old, awesome Italian restaurants, with heaping portions, maps of Italy on the walls, and lots of cops chowing down, which is always a sign of killer food! Miceli's has a piano bar with live lounge music and special jazz shows with guest singers. I've seen Julia Roberts there twice, for whatever that's worth... A well-kept neighborhood secret is **Huston's Texas Pit Bar-B-Que** (1620 Cahuenga, 1/2 block south of Hollywood Blvd.; 323-464-3972). *Everyone* eats here, sitting at Formica tables, with coleslaw and hot sauce dribbling down their chins. It's awesome! Just down the street from Huston's is a cool hair salon, **Hairroin** (1553 Caheunga, 323-467-0392) where you can get yo' hair did, or your face on — and right up the street is **Beauty Bar** (1638 Cahuenga, 323-464-7676), a watering hole done up like a retro beauty parlor. During their Happy Hour you can relax with a martini and get your nails done! The three blocks of Cahuenga between Franklin and Sunset, by the way, are chock full o'trendy clubs and bars, including the **Burgundy Room,** the **Hotel Café,** the **Velvet Margarita** (which also has dynamite Mexican food), **White Lotus**, **XES** and more... check *LA Weekly* listings for what's happening.

During the day, for a panoramic view of the famous **Hollywood Sign**, drive north on Beachwood from Franklin Avenue, and it will be there, right in front of you, rising from the hills. You can't get up to it without hiking for, like, three hours through brush and fire trails (definitely not recommended — not just because of snakes and bad terrain — but because you'll probably get popped for trespassing) but you can turn left onto Ledgewood Drive, then right on DeRonda and continue up, up, up, to a great viewpoint, suitable for a Hollywood photo-op.

If you want to get all *Brokeback Mountain* (without the hot boy-on-boy action), mosey on up to **Sunset Ranch** (3400 Beachwood, 323-469-5450, www.sunsetranchhollywood.com) and go horseback riding through the hills of Griffith Park. They rent horses (for riders of all levels) and offer a terrific moonlight ride down the hill into Burbank, culminating in a Mexican dinner; they also offer private night rides with a ten-person minimum, horse boarding, and riding lessons.

The **Beachwood Cafe** is located on Beachwood just inside the gates of **Hollywoodland**: twin stone towers left over from the '20s when the entire area was real estate development — later they dropped the 'land' and it became plain old Hollywood. This coffeeshop is homey and cute, with gigantic portions of comfort food, malts, a few concessions to nouvelle cuisine, and patrons who "take meetings" in expensive sweats, fresh from yoga class.

If you cruise some of the other main drags in Hollywood, there's more cool stuff. On Highland, just south of Sunset (and down the street from Hollywood High), is **Retropia** (1443 N. Highland Ave., 323-871-4001, www.retropia.net), a fantastic vintage furniture shop which also holds art shows run by debonair deejay-about-town Senor Amor. Another guy with a big local rep is Bob Roberts, a world-famous tattoo artist. He and his son Charlie run **Spotlight Tattoos** (5859 Melrose Ave., 323-871-1084). Elevating tattoos to fine art, this is one of the oldest established shops in the area, and they do fine work. Make an appointment.

A bit farther west, Melrose Avenue turns into a trendy, alternative, youth-centric 'hood, akin to the Harajuku district of Tokyo or London's Carnaby Street in the Swingin' '60s. Melrose was pioneered in the mid-to-late '70s by Billy Shire, owner of **La Luz De Jesus Gallery** and **Wacko** (now located at 4633 Hollywood Blvd., 323-663-0122, laluzdejesus.com). This gallery and combo book/toy/cosmetics and knick-knack superstore is kinda like the great ancestor to every boutique on Melrose, as is vintage emporium the **Aardvark's Odd Ark** (7579 Melrose, 310-655-6769).

On the stretch bordered by La Brea on the east and Fairfax on the West, Melrose is jam-packed with adorable shops, hair salons, cafes, and galleries, including **Squaresville** and **Wasteland** (both vintage), **Urban Outfitters, Jamba Juice**, **Thirteen BC** (spotless piercing studio with beautiful, custom-made jewelry), **Camden Lock** (poppy, punky designer clothes), **Maya** (gorgeous jewelry and accessories), **Chic-A-Boom** (vintage toys, furniture, jewelry, collectibles), and literally dozens more fabulous shops. Go explore!

There are a couple of neighborhoods that'd be good for a full afternoon or evening date where you won't need a car... everything you could possibly want to do is within a couple of blocks. One is the **Franklin Strip** — Franklin Ave. between Tamarind and Canyon Drive. The tiny **Upright Citizens Brigade Theater** (5919 Franklin, 323-908-8702) hosts comedy improv and one-act plays; **Birds** (5925 Franklin, 323-908-8702), a great place for chicken, wraps, and snacks with a full bar and a hopping neighborhood scene after dark; **Pimai Thai Cuisine** (5833 Franklin Ave, 323-461-7841); **Video Hut** (1931 N. Bronson Ave); and **Counterpoint Records** (5911 Franklin Ave., 323-469-4465 www.counterpointbooks andrecords.com), which houses a huge stock of new and used vinyl, CDs, cassettes, and books. The adjacent **Harmony Gallery** (www.harmonygallery.com) features art by people like ex-Warhol superstar Mary Woronov, and regular readings by the likes of Lydia Lunch, Jerry Stahl, Lily Burana, and touring authors. Very cool. Just next door is the shabby-chic delicious French bistro, **La Poubelle**. There's also **Victor's Spirits** (1915 N. Bronson Ave., 323-464-0275), a gourmet wine shop that delivers; they also own a gourmet deli next door, **Victor's**, a *very* popular lunch spot.

The other cool strip to wander — though it's not nearly as big — is Vermont Avenue between Hollywood and Franklin, in Los Feliz. A really popular hang is **Fred's 62** (1850 N. Vermont, 323-667-0062), a retro-looking diner that serves really healthy, vaguely Asian-tinged coffeeshop food, and stays open to the wee hours. One of the best vintage shops on this strip is another branch of **Squaresville** (1800 N. Vermont, 323-669-8464), which is always getting new stock and does trades as well as selling and buying clothes. **Y-Que** (1770 N. Vermont, 323-664-0021) is a hot little knick-knack shop with objets d'art, handmade and ethnic jewelry, stickers, candles... a good place for gift-buying. The **Los Feliz Theater** (1822 N. Vermont Ave.) has current movies as well as art films with bargain matinees, and right next door is **Mako**, a dirt-cheap and scrumptious Japanese restaurant. **Skylight Books** (1816-1/2 N. Vermont, 323-660-1175) is huge and sunny, with mind-boggling selections from the classics to hard-to-get fanzines. They regularly host high profile readings and book-signings. Check out their most-loved staff member- it's Lucy, the orange tabby cat who is usually found lounging in the window! Right next door is the **Skylight Theater**, where you can see plays, and next door to that is **La La Ling,** a kid'n'baby boutique that has adorable stuff but it shockingly over-priced. The **Dresden Room** (1760 N. Vermont, 323-665-4294) was popularized by the movie *Swingers* but has been a popular watering hole since the early '60s, and still features the campy husband and wife duo of Marty and Elayne, who wear matching his 'n' her sparkly outfits and do lounge numbers and show tunes five nights a week. The bar area is cozy and always jammed, and there's a futuristic dining room in the back with plush, off-white tuck 'n' roll booths where you can order the Dresden's cholesterol-laden but invariably delish fare, like deep-fried stuffed mushroom caps. Along this part of Vermont, there's also a post office, a couple of tattoo shops, a Greek place, and a great taco stand/car-wash with a **Starbucks** right near it.

And just down the street are **Barnsdall Park**, which in addition to nice grounds and art galleries, hosts kids' classes and performance programs, has an auditorium, and Frank Lloyd Wright's magnificent **Hollyhock House**.

Tired from running around? I saved the best for last. My favorite thing on the face of the earth — well, one of them, anyway — is the rosewater sorbet at **Mashti Malone's** (1525 N. La Brea Ave., 323-874-0146). This Persian ice cream parlor makes their own frozen delicacies: creamy confections of pistachio, coconut, chocolate and nougat, you name it. But their rosewater sorbet is like eating a mouthful of chilly, perfumed crystal flowers. Pour sour cherry syrup on it, squeeze in a few drops of fresh lemon, and you'll be in heaven, I swear.

Please believe that I could go on and on about things to see and do in Los Feliz, let alone Hollywood. You just must hit the streets. Now get your explorations started!

FABULOUS DOWNTOWN L.A.
Margaret Cho

Los Angeles is where I have made my home, and my favorite places in the city are all Downtown. "Downtown" isn't really the proper thing to call it, because LA is hardly a town, more like a series of cities pressed into a cluster, held together by crowded, broken windshieldglass-strewn freeways and neighborhoods so different they don't even seem like they are in the same country, much less the same city. Downtown LA is as city as the city can get, with lots of places to buy counterfeit merchandise and fairly low-grade recreational drugs. But I am not usually in the market for those things. My addictions are far simpler and much easier to authenticate.

I love fabric, and the best place to start is **Michael Levine's** (919 So. Maple Ave., 213-622-6259) on Maple at 8th. This landmark store has three locations on Maple: the main store, the home décor/upholstery store across the street, and the Annex, which is just upstairs from that. I've never been to the Annex, because it feels sordid to buy fabric by the pound, but that is just me, and remember, fortune favors the brave.

A word of warning: **Michael Levine's** has its own parking lot, which looks tempting because there is almost never any street parking (and if there is, there is a meter which will charge you a quarter every fifteen seconds or something unless you can find a homeless person to jam it for you). If you do acquire the services of a homeless person, it is only proper to give them the same amount you might have spent on the meter itself. That is just fair trade. It is better not to risk the vicious meter men and maids on bikes who patrol the area with a vigilance not seen since Salem in the 1700s and issue tickets like it is the last day of the month every single day. Find a garage to park in. They are all over the place, and will cost around $5-6. Although **Michael Levine's** lot is supposedly free with validation, the stamp only comes with a $20 purchase, and you are only given one hour of free parking. After that, the rate goes to an absurdly high figure, and cannot be negotiated down in any way. *Just don't park there.* **Michael Levine's** will take more than an hour, no matter what you are looking for. It is a wonderland, an incredible, endless sea of fabrics, notions, patterns, feathers, buttons, yarn — everything for the home sewer and the trade. The prices aren't cheap, and you will often find better bargains in the smaller stores on the surrounding streets. They do sell wholesale, which makes the prices a little better, but you have to have a resale number. Retail or wholesale, the service is the same. Really, really slow. Like way more than an hour. I think that even though this is THE fabric capital of Los Angeles, the employees seem to only have one pair of scissors to cut yardage, and they belong to the one lady who is perpetually on break. The lines to get fabric cut are long, and can get nasty. Never underestimate the irritability and short fuse of someone with the need to make their own clothes.

Even though you will probably have to wait awhile, don't even think about using the bathroom, which will cost you a quarter if it is even open which is rare, and you absolutely HAVE to, but really, try to hold it. There is no toilet seat. There is nowhere for people to aim. There are so many weird stains and no seat covers that if you must go, you have to hang off the edge with the deft mastery of an ancient yogi. If you aren't a steady practitioner of TM, on your way to learning how to levitate, don't bother. That is all I can say about it. It is literally the worst toilet in the Americas.

Actually, this is a very important point to remember about Downtown LA... There is NOWHERE to go to the bathroom, which makes it an inappropriate place to bring children, the elderly, the PMS-ing, dieters, pretty much anyone without a solid steel bladder or already wearing adult diapers. Even restaurants will not allow you to use theirs before — or after — you have eaten in them. I just try to avoid liquids before I go, and then make my excursions quick and uncomplicated. It is the only way.

The **Michael Levine's home décor** store is usually quiet, but it doesn't have as much variety, although the trim can be beautiful and outrageous. The good news is, all goes on sale eventually, but you have to wait a very long time. After **Michael Levine's**, the best fabric stores are concentrated around Maple and 8th. Going toward 7th on Maple, you have **Beads and Trim** (820-2 S. Maple Ave., 213-622-6220), which is my favorite, and the best beads on the block at **Bohemian Crystal Bead Factory**, (812 Maple Ave., 213-627-9553, www.beadsfactory.com) which is expensive but worth it.

Berger Beads is on 7th, and also extraordinary but closed on Sundays.

I get hungry and hot fairly fast because, even if you wear a hat, the sidewalk will blast back the unforgiving Southern California sun right into your face. I will usually stop for a treat, usually in the form of a nice, ripe mango, dipped in lime juice, salt and chili powder, sold by **cart vendors** all over the street. I haven't tried the other fruit, which depending on the season can be watermelon, pineapple, cucumber — I guess technically a fruit — but I always get the mango because it is just so delicious. It is sweet, sour, salty, spicy... the only thing it isn't is bitter, but you still use almost your whole tongue to taste it. It comes in a plastic bag with a tiny napkin square, and it will get all over your hands and don't even think about bringing it into a store. It's always market price, about $2. There is also a great **Korean restaurant** on Maple between 7th and 8th, but remember, *they don't have a restroom.*

If you aren't a seamstress or a, uh, seamster, Downtown still has much to offer. **Santee Alley** is just a block and a half up from Michael Levine's and it has some of the best clothing bargains in all of Los Angeles. You can shop for the latest knockoff handbags, shoes, jeans, hoodies, belt buckles, you name it. Some of the most beautiful items in my closet are from **Santee Alley**, but the quality isn't always very controlled, so check for dyes that run and make you look like you have gray skin or really dirty fingernails, burst seams, and overall shoddy craftsmanship. Also, the best merchandise isn't displayed on the gorgeous bubble-butted mannequins, so it really pays to look around (check out **Axxent**, 1008 S. Santee St. #A, 213-745-7963).

Off **Santee Alley**, there are lots of fantastic stores specializing in accessories. On **Olympic**, there are stores that sell every kind of rhinestone bauble you can think of, like bright butterflies and jeweled snake barrettes to hold up your hair, and of course I have to have them in every color. They are too heavy to actually wear on your head without stressing the follicles, but what a lovely mess they make in the bathroom cabinets! More jewelry than can be worn in one lifetime! Tiny purses that are only able to carry one OB tampon! There is everything! There is anything! A shopping addict's paradise! Again, quality varies. Watch out for rhinestone fallout! It is dangerous! I bought a very charming handbag with a rhinestone buckle, and on its first night out, the stones fell out of their settings and left long, jagged cuts in my thumb and fingertips, and no matter how cute they are to begin with, nobody likes a bloody purse unless you are perhaps a boxer. I am many things but I am not a pugilist and fucking up your fingertips is king amongst the small injuries. I threw the offending handbag away, but the wounds took a long time to heal, and now I look upon rhinestones as a potential enemy rather than a glamorous friend.(**Beacon Belts'n'Buckles**, 310 E. Olympic Blvd., 323-580-9707)

If you tire of shopping, or you really can't hold it anymore, then Olympic will lead you right to **Olympic Spa** (3915 W. Olympic Blvd, 323-857-0666, www.olympicspala.com), in the heart of glorious Koreatown. Olympic Spa has fulfilled all of my hammam fantasies, and has everything but the eunuch, with a long and detailed menu of fantastic treatments, which all include unlimited use of the jade steam room, showers, hot and cold pools, the sauna and the too-hot-to-handle mugwort tea bath. The treatments are sensibly priced and incredibly relaxing. I love the thorough Korean style (i.e., almost painful) body scrub, the deep tissue massage, the firming facial, the vigorous scalp massage and accompanying shampoo and conditioning rinse which you can buy in a package with a variety of other little treats and fancies, all administered by a very able-bodied nice Korean lady dressed in a conical black bra and high-waisted panties. It's the best spa deal in town, and they even have a restaurant, but unfortunately the whole spa is ladies only, and don't even try to bring eggs in there. A sign actually tells you not to.

Also Recommended:

Button and Trim Expo, 828 Maple Ave., 213-622-2323

Fiesta Fabric, 850 S. Maple Ave., 213-891-0148

Fabrics & Fabrics, 403 E. 9th St., 213-488-0681

Trim, 820-9 Maple Ave., 213-489-1223

Elegance Fashion Mart Inc., 124 E. Olympic Blvd. #100, 213-743-9119

W&P Trading Co., 1031 S. Los Angeles St., 213-765-0680

Top 2 Toe , 1023 S. Maple Ave (alley), 213-746-1646

Exploring Downtown LA, MacArthur Park + Koreatown

Culture

Museum of Contemporary Art (MOCA) (250 S. Grand Ave., 213-626-6222, www.moca.org) Awesome museum, with permanent exhibits and rotating collections of modern art. They've had great shows, including a retrospective of punk-era posters and comics, etc by Raymond Pettibone, whose work you may recognize from Black Flag covers... their companion museum is the **Geffen Contemporary** (152 N. Central Ave, same website and phone) which is just a couple of blocks away. housed in a former police car garage.

Museum of Neon Art (501 W. Olympic Blvd., 213-489-9918, www.mona.net) Everything you ever wanted in artistic neon... with a hip twist. They once even did an exhibit of art from Burning Man. They also offer classes.

Chinatown (Broadway and side streets between Sunset and Alpine) Many awesome restaurants, hundreds of Asian souvenir stores, groceries and places to get acupuncture and Chinese herbs; and lately, many indie art galleries.

Millennium Biltmore Hotel (506 S. Grand Ave., 213-624-1011, www.milleniumhotels.com) Gorgeously kept up, you can step back into another more genteel era here. The Biltmore's lobby was also the last place Elizabeth Short (The Black Dahlia) was seen alive. Have a cocktail in her honor and soak up a bit of Old Hollywood history. You have probably seen this amazing building in *Chinatown, Ghostbusters*, and *The Pink Panther* though it's even more stunning in real life.

Eats

Langer's Deli (704 South Alvarado, 213-483-8050) A classic, old school deli with AWESOME pastrami sandwiches, just across the street from MacArthur Park, which used to be dangerous day and night, and is now (slightly) cleaned up... but still, don't go there after dark, unless, of course, you wanna buy a balloon of Mexican heroin. While you're on Alvarado, you may want to check out the crazy swap meets, piñata stores, street vendors and botanicas between 6th and 8th Streets.

Taylor's Steak House (3361 W. 8th St., 213-382-8449) perfectly preserved Swingin' '60s steakhouse. Chomp down on fat, reasonably-priced steaks, chops and prime rib, down a martini and relax in the huge burgundy tuck 'n' roll booths.

Drinks

The Golden Gopher (417 W. 8th St., 213-876-7651) One of the oldest bars in the city also holds one of the oldest liquor licenses in LA—which means that they have their very own package store inside, for your carry-out booze needs. No longer a dive, the Gopher is now a hipster hang, and regularly packed.

LA BOHEME
Silver Lake and Echo Park
Andrea Ferrante

So you want to get a taste of *La Vie Bohéme*? Cruise Sunset Blvd. towards downtown: once you cross Hillhurst, the grittiness of East Hollywood starts to ease. The strip malls give way to small storefronts, quaint architecture, succulent greenery, and undulating hills full of palm trees. The heady scent of tropical flowers in bloom mixes with that of the late night taqueria on the corner, cars zig-zag up narrow winding streets, and the whole place can take on the feeling of a noir film come dusk. Welcome to LA's version of the Left Bank.

When local residents like Beck and Elliott Smith drew attention to the vibrant music scene, Silver Lake and its residents got labeled the hippest 'hood in town which consequently sent the area's real estate skyrocketing. Echo Park followed suit shortly. Even with the proliferation of trendy boutiques and increasingly expensive restaurants, there are still discoveries to be made and the overall effect remains charming yet livable. Within its boundaries lie some of the loveliest examples of late-19th to mid-20th century architecture and parks in the city. Not only does Silver Lake contain a liberal dose of avant-garde gems by greats such as Gregory Ain and Richard Neutra, but there are also sprinkles of tiny bungalows. storybook cottages, and campy '50s dingbats throughout the hillsides. Echo Park's **Angelino Heights** boasts the largest remaining concentration of Victorians, many of which have recently been restored. These sit tete-a-tete with the many cafés, restaurants, bars, antique shops, hip ateliers, and cultural centers that make this area unusually walkable for LA.

Whether hiking and biking through **Elysian Park**, loitering beside the fresh fruit carts and taco stands at Sunset and Echo Park Ave, running with the pack at the **Silver Lake Dog Park**, or paddling a boat around **Echo Park Lake**, locals like to soak up the sunshine and cultural vibrancy that surrounds them. On a clear, warm day, the area seems to pulsate with a shimmering glow: if you find yourself atop Angelino Heights during one of those wondrous nuclear sunsets LA is famous for, you might conclude that occasional wheezing is a small price to pay for such an appealing mix of urbanity and natural beauty.

SUNSET JUNCTION

The unofficial gateway to Silver Lake is known as **Sunset Junction** and is marked by the faded beauty of the **Vista Theater** (4473 W. Sunset, 323-660-6639), a one-screen throwback to a grander time, featuring a mix of artsy-indie flicks as well as edgy blockbusters. Across from the Vista is **Uncle Jer's** (4459 W. Sunset, 323-662-6710), a hodgepodge of ethnic goods, flowing Bollywood skirts, and cute tchotchkes, cards and candles. At **Rudy's Barbershop** (4451 W. Sunset, 323-661-6535, www.rudysbarbershop.com), you can get a cheap walk-in cut from a hip stylist for about $22. Check out their selection of hair products, or flick through the hip art mags for sale while you wait. If your new 'do is not to your liking, drown your sorrows over at **Tiki Ti** (4427 W. Sunset, 213-669-9381, www.tiki-ti.com). Slap your cash on the table for their big tropical drinks with chunks of fruit and cute little parasols. If you're overwhelmed by the 80+ choices, then spin the big drink roulette wheel. Don't even think about trying to order a beer 'cause they don't serve any!

Stroll down a few blocks and arrive at the heart of the junction. If it's nighttime, then it's the right time for **Akbar** (4356 W. Sunset, 323-665-6810), a straight-friendly gay bar with an anything-goes clientele. Their strong drinks and rockin' jukebox make this my favorite place to sling back a few amongst close friends. Or just make some new ones by seeing how many people you can squeeze into their tiny men's urinal!

If you happen to make it out before last call, (Editors' note: a near impossibility), stumble across the way to **Circus of Books** (4001 W. Sunset, 323-666-1304, www.circusof books.com). Open till 2 a.m. every night to service fashion-mag, bad porno, and trashy midnight-snack needs. From lube and condoms to a wide variety of smoking paraphernalia, they've got your vices covered.

When you've watched the sun come up to the sound of Arabic pop music and you need a chill place to start your day, then "come to zeee Casbahhh." The **Casbah Cafe** (3900 W. Sunset, 323-664-7000) is the perfect place to don some dark sunglasses and soak up that Euro-boho vibe. This French/Moroccan corner spot is perfect for a *petit dejeuner* and people watching, or a small pot of tea with a handful of dates and fresh cherries. If you can afford to take home some of their fluffy Turkish towels, lovely tapestries, and Moroccan slippers, your pad will feel like a souk in no time. If we're talking recovery from serious overindulgence, the kind that lands you in the second and third levels of Dante's *Inferno*, then hurry over to **Prasada** (3818 W. Sunset, 323-644-0068) and redeem yourself. This humble temple to "health, balance, and decadence" is a welcome retreat from the hustle and bustle of the main drag. The last time I stopped in, there was some fine bluegrass playing as I sipped my "liquid divinity" (a fresh, organic blend of orange juice, banana and ginger). Try one of the "rejuvenating" salads or their house specialty, a carrot-cardamom-almond shake. Lots of choices for omnivores and vegans alike, so repent sinners, repent!

FURTHER INTO SILVER LAKE

There are two or three main drags in Silver Lake: Sunset, as well as the Hyperion/Rowena/Glendale corridor, and Silver Lake Blvd itself. Get out and explore. A leisurely afternoon could be spent along any of these stretches. Or, if coming from another part of town, eat, drink, and shop your way around the entire loop.

Food and Drink

KP's Vietnamese Deli (2616 Hyperion, 323-913-1818, www.kpsdeli.com) This tiny place rocks for lunch! KP's is known for their delicious *Banh Mi*, long Vietnamese sandwiches on French rolls that can easily feed two people. Carnivores have got to try KP's special Kold Kut with several kinds of meat and paté, and they have a veggie version also. In a hurry? Just call in your order and they'll bring it to the curb when you honk! Did I mention the yummy drinks and free wireless, too?

Zanzabelle (2912 Rowena Ave., 323-663-9900) Pull over when you see the giant giraffe because this delightful sweet-shoppe has something with your name on it. Featuring old-fashioned candies, chocolate bars, and sodas, as well as Dr. Bob's rich ice cream in gourmet flavors. Quaint children's toys and novelties, too!

Edendale Grill (2838 Rowena Ave., 323-666-2000, www.edendalegrill.com) Patti Peck, former owner of Millie's Diner, has converted old Fire Station 56 into a swank American bistro and bar, open for dinner and Sunday brunch. Try the Caesar Salad for two, prepared tableside from the original Mexican recipe. Then kick it with a cocktail from the Mixville Bar (formerly the fire truck bay) on one of their patios. Don't miss the old-school (and working) black and white photobooth on the back patio and the historical old Hollywood prints in the lobby!

Red Lion Tavern (2366 Glendale, 323-662-5337) A Bavarian -style beer hall with frauleins in dirndls, red tuck'n'roll booths, a garden patio and authentic (i.e., heavy meat-laden) German food.

Jade Café (1521 Griffith Park Blvd., 323-667-1551, www.jadecafe.org) Completely organic raw food fusion comes to the Eastside, at reasonable prices. Creative preparation and presentation, and so damn yummy!

Millie's Diner (3524 W. Sunset, 323-664-0404) Though Keith Morris from the Circle Jerks no longer waits on the locals and Bob Forrest from Thelonious Monster is no longer washing the dishes, Millie's is still a Silver Lake institution, and also where you'll find me chowing down on Saturday afternoons. Our charming editors, Iris, used to work there, and Plez loves to devour the Jackie G special with extra hot sauce, while I love the homemade biscuits with mushroom gravy.

Alegria (3510 W. Sunset, 323-913-1422, www.Alegria OnSunset.com) Brightly colored walls and Frida Kahlo-inspired art adorn this bright Mexican café, but the locals stand in line for the food. Their molé is delicious and if you like coffee, don't dare miss the *Café de la Olla*. Cash only.

Café Tropical (2900 W. Sunset, 323-661-8391) For more than 30 years, the corner of Sunset and Parkman has been home to this warm and inviting slice of Cuba. The light green walls are lined with pictures of Che Guevera, brightly colored paper lanterns dangle from the ceiling, and the long wood counter always boasts fresh flowers. Known for their reasonable prices, strong *espresso con leche*, grilled Cuban-style sandwiches and their signature guava-cheese pie, Tropical has both the locals and would-be revolutionaries singing their praises. It's also the "happening" AA hot spot.

Pho Café (2841 W. Sunset, 213-413-0888) Also known as "No Name Pho" due to their lack of a sign, this little gem tucked into a strip mall serves up satisfying bowls of Vietnamese soup as well as spring rolls, vermicelli noodle dishes, and beer. Suck it up. Open 'til midnight. Cash only.

Mae Ploy (2606 W. Sunset, 213-353-9635) This is where I stop before my belly dance class (held at Studio With No Name, coincidentally right across the street from No Name Pho) to fuel up on Thai iced tea, and often where I end up afterwards for the tasty food. Super friendly place that makes you feel like family by your second visit.

Bars, Nightlife, and Culture

El Cid (4212 W. Sunset, 323-668-0357, elcidla.com) This replica of a 16th century Spanish Tavern is worth checking out for its somewhat "pricey, but worth it" Flamenco Shows, and recently revamped menu of Spanish food. The building was also the first soundstage in Hollywood movie history. In addition to Flamenco, they now feature burlesque and comedy nights, as well as salsa dancing and live bands.

Ghetto Gloss Gallery (2380 Glendale Blvd, 323-912-0008, www.ghettogloss.com) Half gallery/half pop-culture shop, Ghetto Gloss stocks one of the best selections of indie-weird books in town, as well as zines, clothing by Cyrus & Sonny and a PBR vending machine. Past art shows have included works by Dr. Kevorkian, Moon Zappa, and Annie Sperling. Get on their list and ghett-down with the Gloss!

Silver Lake Lounge (2906 W. Sunset, 323-663-9636, www.foldsilverlake.com) Rock bands during the week and Hispanic drag shows Friday and Saturdays. Cash only.

Spaceland (1717 Silver Lake Blvd., 323-661-4380, www.clubspaceland.com) The club that put the Silver Lake scene on the map, is still the best place to check out the next wave, with live music almost every night of the week. Mondays usually feature a cool band for free.

Silver Lake Conservatory of Music (3920 Sunset, 323-665-3363, silverlakeconservatory.com) Founded by Flea from the Red Hot Chili Peppers in 2001, this non-profit organization is one of the community's real jewels. Featuring eight sound-proof rooms for practicing, affordable music lessons with excellent teachers (mostly LA legends like pianist Zachary Gertzman), plus scholarships for low-income children.

Jeff Electric Gallery (3022 W. Sunset, 323-664-8580, www.jeffelectricgallery.com) Most days this space serves as the home office for his electrical business, but every couple of months, his stuff gets tucked away while he and his sister hang their favorite local artists and throw a big shindig. Check out the site and get on his list.

Shopping and Services

Rosemary's Billygoat Odditorium (4519 Sunset, 323-666-GOAT, www.rosemarysbillygoat.com) While technically just on the other side of Virgil in Hollywood, this place's oddball aesthetic screams "Eastside." Named after the proprietor's prop-rock band of the same name, its facade leers like something from a carny sideshow. Inside, this dark cavern is filled with taxidermy animal heads, bone sculptures, creepy dollies, edgy paintings, post-punk crafty clothing, plus occult supplies by Black Broom. They host the occasional live show and cabaret. Spooky-ooky-kooky...

Come to Mama's (4019 W. Sunset, 323-953-1275) The place for funky '60s/'70s pieces and vintage hand-dyed slips and petticoats.

Maker (4008 Santa Monica Blvd., 323-662-2524) No words can adequately describe the creative madness that is Maker. Functional art, handmade with love. Open when they feel like it, but weekends are usually a good bet!

American Electric Tattoo (3532 W. Sunset, 323-664-6530, www.americanelectrictattoo.com) Come on in and let proprietor Craig Jackman regale you with funny road stories — you may recognize him from his popular band Throw Rag — while he and his crew drill some custom ink into your flesh. Check out his taxidermy collection.

Sweet Charity (3318 W. Sunset, 323-644-8861) A bit pricey, but if you've got the cash to spend on cheeky clothing by young designers, they'll donate 10% of the sale to your choice of six charities.

Bittersweet Butterfly (1406 Micheltorena, 323-660-4303, www.butterflyflowersla.com) Add one generous helping of artful flowers to one dash of sophisticated lingerie and you get this tiny mulberry-colored shop that has your high-femme needs covered. Marie-Belle chocolate, beautiful floral arrangements and gift baskets, sassy sock-garters, and a nice selection of fine European "smalls" make this a place to keep in your little black moleskin. Ooh la-la.

Seven Crows Bookstore (2388 Glendale Blvd., 323-913-9677, www.sevencrowsbooks.com) I recently discovered this used bookshop and its great selection of literary fiction, history, and topics of local interest.

Panty Raid (2378-1/2 Glendale Blvd., 323-668-1888, www.pantyraidshop.com) Home of the Valentine's Day "Panty Gram"! A selection of lingerie from Mary Green, Jezebel, and Hanky Panky. And if you've decided to torture your beau by dragging him along, the PR girls have taken pity on him: they hooked up a Playstation console to distract him from all the fleshy delights behind those dressing room curtains.

Rockaway Records (2395 Glendale Blvd., 323-664-3232, www.rockaway.com) The only record store in Silver Lake is all about collectibles. Whether you want to scoop old issues of *Hullabaloo* or sell your KISS boardgame, peruse the assortment of psychedelic posters and backstage passes, or the biggest selection of Beatles paraphernalia in town, this place is for the record geek in all of us.

Still Yoga (behind Rockaway, 323-906-8960, www.allstill.com) An Anusara yoga studio in the heart of the hood. First class is on the house, so go get bendy.

Outdoors

Sunset Junction Farmers Market (Corner of Edgecliffe and Maltman, just off Sunset, Saturdays 8 a.m.-1 p.m.) Munch on crepes and fresh juice while shopping for fresh produce and flowers.

Neutra Houses Several examples on the 2200 block of Silver Lake Blvd., as well as the 2400 block of Earl Street.

Silver Lake Dog Park (1850 Silver Lake Blvd., at Easterly Terrace) Located at the southern end of the Reservoir, this small park has benches, bags for scooping-the-poop, and even a doggie drinking fountain. (Editors' note: also known to locals as a hot pick-up spot and movie industry, networking hang.)

ECHO PARK

In the early days of the film industry, many of the studios were located here and in an area slightly to the northwest originally known as Edendale. The sunny weather and scenic beauty attracted film companies like Selig, Bison, and even Walt Disney. Laurel and Hardy's slapstick routines were often shot amongst the hills and staircases of the neighborhood, and in the 1960s parts of "Gilligan's Island" were filmed here as well. Lovely ladies such as Pola Negri, Gloria Swanson, and Dolores del Rio were all residents. Before WWII, it was also known as "Red Hill" because of the large concentration of political activists and communists that lived in the area. Later, many Chinese immigrants relocated from nearby Chinatown, and Asian and Pacific Island culture is celebrated every summer at the **Lotus Festival** at Echo Park Lake.

Living up to its bohemian reputation, Echo Park doesn't really get moving until close to 11 or noon, with a few notable exceptions. The odd early birds can go fuel up with the laidback baristas at **Chango** (1559 Echo Park Ave., 213-977-9161, www.changocoffee.com), which opens at 5:30 a.m. during the week. Featuring delicious scones, croissants, and muffins from Susina Bakery as well as Tealogy teas, it is where many locals start their day. If it's past noon, try some yummy ice cream, or their mint lemonade - perfect for the sweltering LA heat. Interesting art, a board for local events, and free wireless after noon, make for a real community space where everybody knows your name.

When it's time to look the part, head next door to **Flounce Vintage** (1550 Echo Park Ave., 213-481-1975, www.flounce vintage.com) They stock Victorian dresses and '70s jumpers, with some sultry '30s lingerie thrown in for good measure. A small section of menswear, plus fabulous shoes and accessories, round out the offerings. While most of the original galleries have moved to more trafficked areas, **Showpony** (1543 Echo Park, 213-482-7676), the darling of the block, is still there wowing the cute'n'crafty set. Stop in for charming, retooled vintage and homespun one-offs by local gals. Coo over owner Kime Buzelli's watercolors of waifs, inspired by witty one-liners from '80s songs. They have openings once a month where they change up the art and there are often cupcakes involved! Open when they feel like it, like most of the neighborhood.

Food and Drink

Brite Spot (1918 W. Sunset, 213-484-9801) This place is best for breakfast, as well as any other time of day or night you've got a hankering for diner food with a twist. Very veggie friendly and open till 4 a.m. on the weekends.

Downbeat Café (1202 N. Alvarado St., 213-483-3955, www.thedownbeatcafe.com) A café done right: old thrift-store couches and Formica tables with '50s chairs, strong iced tea, delicious sandwiches and Billie Holiday crooning on the stereo. Check out their collection of framed vintage *Down Beat* magazines on the wall or the boutique at the bottom of the stairs (which seems to change names and proprietors at least once a year).

Tribal Café (1651 W. Temple, 213-483-4458, www.tribalcafe.com) is a funky local spot with a welcoming vibe. Located a little off the main drag, in the Historic Filipino district, this café reflects its neighborhood by featuring snacks like fried pork rinds, Taro boba tea, Saladitos (dried salted plums) and fresh Mexican food. Try their special "Pirate Chai," made with a blend of green tea and molasses, spicy and not too sweet. They also feature fresh juices, delicious grilled sandwiches, and great veggie option. Add the late hours (weekends till 2 a.m.), free wireless internet, and open mic nights every Monday, and you've got a quintessential café.

While you're there, don't miss **Tamales Alberto** (1644 W. Temple, 213-484-4485) across the street, where you can choose from six different fillings. Whether you buy one to eat there, or a dozen to go, it's homemade tamales and nothing but!

Bars, Nightlife, and Culture

The Echo (1822 W. Sunset, 213-413-8200, www.atthe echo.com) From old school punk to electro-funk, the Echo has a night for anyone that loves to hear new music, including the popular dancehall-themed Dub Club. The kitchen turns out cheap eats and there's a cool patio out back that feels like the smoking section of your high school quad.

Short Stop (1455 W. Sunset, 213-482-4942) Besides a laid-back clientele and stiff drinks, the thing that keeps me coming back is the fact that this ex-cop bar, like the Edendale, has a black & white photo booth!

Little Joy Jr. (1477 W. Sunset, 213-250-3417) This locals dive has cute bartenders, a pool table, and decent drinks as well as an artsy mixed crowd. Cash only.

Echo Park Film Center (1200 N. Alvarado St., 213-484-8846, www.echoparkfilmcenter.org) The place to go for all your "micro-cinema" needs. You can catch one of their regular screenings, take a filmmaking class, buy some Super-8 film or check out something from their cool film and book library. They also sell & rent equipment and do some repairs.

Machine Project (1200 N. Alvarado St., 213-483-8761, www.machineproject.com) This inspiring and ambitious gallery/educational space focuses on where technology and the arts intersect. By hosting workshops, installations, events, and performances they bring together poets, scientists, artists and the greater community to document what happens when these worlds collide. Open weekends.

Shopping and Services

Fashions of Echo Park (1600 W. Sunset, 213-482-1723) Where all the cute cholitas in *Mi Vida Loca* must have gotten their clothes. Trendy but wearable street-styles for budget conscious cuties. (Editors' note: some people like designer labels but Fashions of Echo Park is better.)

Sea Level Records (1716 W. Sunset, 213-989-0146, www.sealevelechopark.com) Not only a great little indie record shop in the shadow of the Jensen Arts building, but they have regular in-store shows as well. Flip through their vinyl while hearing the next big thing for free!

Outdoors

Echo Park has quite a few stunning staircases adorning its hills that remind one that this used to be a somewhat rural area, designed for a different way of life. The most rewarding of these is the **Baxter Stairway** (Baxter Street, three blocks east of Echo Park Ave), which climbs straight up over 200 steps leaving you breathless in both senses of the word. The top of the stairs spits you out across from **Elysian Park**, an oft-overlooked gem (where I've experienced some of my favorite picnics), and plenty more trails to explore. **Laveta Terrace Stairway** (one block east of Echo Park Ave., north of

Sunset) has a wider design with multiple landings to let you rest a bit before making your way to the row of palm trees that awaits at the top.

Elysian Park (1880 Academy Dr., 213-222-9136) The second largest city park in LA has close to 600 acres of hiking trails, picnic areas with barbecue pits, and a children's playground, not to mention **Dodger Stadium.**

Angelino Heights One of the first Los Angeles suburbs, Angelino Heights is best know for its Victorians, especially the beautifully restored Eastlake and Queen Anne houses along the **1300 block of Carroll Avenue**. However, if you drive up and down the streets of the hill, you'll also see a nice array of the Mission Revival, Brownstone, and Streamline Moderne styles. Many Keystone Cops chase scenes were filmed here.

Echo Park Lake (1100 block of Echo Park Ave, between Park and Bellevue) Pack up a picnic lunch and join the scads of families that use the shady slopes as an extension of their yard. Take out a paddleboat and maneuver through the lotus pads that cover parts of the lake. My favorite scenes in *Mi Vida Loca* were filmed here, and there is a beautiful view of the downtown skyline.

FUN IN THE SUN
Exploring the West Side

There's this myth in LA that nothing "cool" ever goes down on the West Side. That the broad avenues of the beach communities are jammed with SUVs driven by delusional *nouveau riche* soccer moms who think that just because they're rockin' a porn-star manicure and co-coordinated Juicy sweats, and can afford a shot of Botox every now and then, people will mistake them for Eva Longoria. Well, okay, maybe that's partly true. But to hear the disdainful conversation at ...oh, any public place from Echo Park to Atwater, you'd think that the West Side was pure poison, a milquetoast suburban sprawl with no redeeming qualities. To most, the West Side means anything from La Cienega to the beaches but some Eastsiders are so adamantly anti-Westside they claim they'd rather die than venture past La Brea! Well, they don't know what they're missing.

A lot of LA history occurred on what is technically "The West Side." Whaddaya think Jan and Dean or the Beach Boys were singing about? Newsflash: it wasn't Silver Lake, pal! And speaking of Jan and Dean, in 1964, they had a Top Ten hit with their song, "Dead Man's Curve". Co-incidentally, one of the most picturesque ways of driving to the beach will have you careening around the stretch of road known locally as **Dead Man's Curve**. If you start out from Hollywood and head west on Sunset, just follow it to the beach, and Pacific Coast Highway. On the way, you'll pass the world-famous **Sunset Strip**. You'll then go through Beverly Hills, and won't be able to miss the **Beverly Hills Hotel**, the monstrous bright pink Art Deco hotel complex on your right amidst the more stately Tudor-style mansions. Sunset will curve a few times, and you will be going slightly uphill. Just before you get to **Bel Air Estates**, there will be a long, steeply banked and very sharp curve — this is it. But the spookiest part is that in 1966, two years after Jan and Dean scored with this song, Jan (full name: Jan Berry, no relation to my co-editor, by the way) wiped out in a fatal crash on the *very same stretch of road*. Berry's Corvette smashed into a parked truck, killing three people. He survived, but barely: he was in a coma for weeks and suffered permanent brain damage.

Okay, on a lighter note: remember those classic movies *The Sting* and *Inside Daisy Clover*? Both were filmed on location at the **Santa Monica Pier** (Ocean and Colorado, Santa Monica, 310-458-8900, www.santamonicapier.org) which still houses the amazing, turn-of-the-century carousel featured in both films — now fully restored to its former glory — as well as souvenir shops, lotsa fast food and carnival-style snacks, free summer concerts, an arcade, kiddie rides, and an amazing aquarium. Visit **Rusty's** (on the Pier, 310-393-7437) for dinner, cocktails, or a quick game of pool. There's also a huge Ferris wheel where, on a clear day, an incredible view of the coast from Hermosa Beach on the south up to the mountains of Malibu is visible. Think of all those Annette Funicello and Frankie Avalon movies... or their modern equivalent, *Baywatch*. They were filmed in Santa Monica, and Venice too, along with Oliver Stone's *The Doors* and more recently, *The Lords of Dogtown*, which traced the history of the Zephyr Team. The Z-Boys, as they were known, included legendary skateboarders Tony Alva, Jay Adams and Stacy Peralta, who irrevocably changed the sport with their daredevil, guerilla stunts... perfected in the streets and alleys of Venice and Ocean Park. And even though it seems lame in contrast to the films just mentioned (which definitely makes it a "guilty pleasure"), *Beverly Hills 90210* was filmed at least partially in Beverly Hills, which qualifies as West Side, ask *anyone*! Oh, and for the record: that also means *The Beverly Hillbillies* took place on the West Side, though in reality, the palatial house that served as the exterior of Jed Clampett's mansion is actually in Bel Air, an exclusive, gated community, also on the West Side.

But even before television or the movies existed, our beaches and their neighboring communities were attractions. In 1904, wealthy businessman and world-traveler Abbot Kinney bought a huge parcel of land south of Ocean Park, and planned to turn it into a resort. He started re-creating Venice, Italy by dredging canals out of the marshland, and on July 4, 1905, the ribbon was cut opening up sixteen miles of the **Venice Canals**. Sadly, by 1929, with the rise of the automobile, many of them were filled in, but quite a few still exist. They used to be a boho enclave full of ramshackle Craftsman bungalows (Jim Morrison lived here) but now, the adorable cottages sit nestled among modern condos and multimillion-dollar mansions. Still, the canals left are fun — and free — to explore. They're full of charm, with their picturesque bridges, rowboats, and shallow waterways populated by families of wild and domestic ducks.

In stark contrast to the tranquil, almost rural, feel of the canals, Venice's **Ocean Front Walk** (which stretches up through Ocean Park all the way to the Santa Monica Pier) is like a surfside circus, open 365 days a year. Locals often refer to it as the **Venice Boardwalk**; even though it's paved: it's more like a crowed, though scenic alley. Check it out live at **www.westland.net/beachcam**. It's the place always seen in cheesy B movie montages when they wanna show some wacky California flavah. The Walk is always full of street performers, with some of the more famous being chainsaw juggler Robert Gruenberg, and the white-clad, turbaned Jimi Hendrix-wannabe Harry Perry, who's been wailing on his axe through a portable amp while roller-skating through the crowds for twenty years. Ocean Front Walk also has dozens of tented swapmeet-style stores, where you can buy sarongs, bikinis, incense, souvenir t-shirts, jewelry, stickers, and vintage clothes. There are also places to rent bikes, surfboards or boogie boards by the day; plenty of cafes ranging from cruddy fast food to healthy gourmet fare. Be prepared for a long wait for tables on weekends or during the warmer months. There's also fortune-tellers, face-painters, hair-braiders, ten dollars-for-ten-minute massages, chalk artists, and, of course, **Muscle Beach**, the iron-pumpin', wave-adjacent outdoor gym where body builders like our fair state's "Governator" got his start.

Venice's **Abbot Kinney Boulevard** is also a great place to get a bite or windowshop after a day wandering the Boardwalk. Take in all the cute boutiques and art shops, or just people-watch in a bar or café. Practically around the corner is **Beyond Baroque Literary Arts Center** (681 Venice Blvd.,

310-822-3006, www.beyondbaroque.org), a fabulous intellectual collective serving the community for decades. It's hosted some amazing authors over the years, as well as the odd concert. It also has a gallery and offers poetry and prose workshops, free open readings, and boasts a great bookstore.

Another fun place to fritter away an afternoon (or a whole day) is Downtown Santa Monica's **Third Street Promenade**. You can't miss it — it's guarded by huge topiary dinosaurs, and takes up most of Third Street. The City of Santa Monica blocked it off to become an open-air pedestrian mall, and it's great. There are many talented street performers, fountains and benches, restaurants with al fresco dining, and a number of stores which encourage browsing. Plenty of public parking nearby... and if the promenade gets too over-populated, sneak around the corner into the cool darkness of **Ye Olde King's Head Pub** (116 Santa Monica Blvd., 310-451-1402, yeoldkingshead pub.com) which is not only a swingin', sometimes-rowdy, authentic English pub, it's also a restaurant. Their fish'n'chips are battered to perfection and meltingly tender. They're also so bleedin' 'uge, they'd feed two, *easy.*

There's a lot of nightlife on the West Side, too. Small, experimental theaters abound, showcasing plays, dramatic readings, performance art, and dance productions. Two of the best are **Highways Performance Space** (1651 18th St., Santa Monica, 310-453-1755, www.highwaysperformance.org) and **The Electric Lodge** (1416 Electric Avenue, Venice, 310-306-1854, www.electriclodge.org). Both are fiercely independent, like to showcase new works and emerging artists, and offer classes and workshops.

If it's music you're after, there are also some cool haunts. **Harvelle's** (1432 4th St., Santa Monica, 310-395-1676, www.harvelles.com) is a venerated venue for blues and jazz; **14 Below** (1348 14th St., Santa Monica, 310-451-5040 often features local alternative bands. **McCabe's Music Store** (3101 Pico Blvd., West LA, 310-828-4403) is not just a music store and a place to get music lessons. For the better part of three decades, it's also held great shows in its intimate back room. World-class country, rock, folk and ethnic musicians play here, as well as the best local singer/ songwriters, and an occasional spoken word show... with folks like Exene Cervenka and Jim Caroll. If ya want to make an evening of it, there's also an incredible Mexican restaurant a mere half-mile away. **The Talpa** (1175 Pico, West LA, 310-478-3353) is classic LA Mexicana, strictly old school: we're talking badly-painted-but-great luridly colored murals, killer amounts of food, and scorching, homemade roasted tomatillo salsa. Talpa also boasts a dark bar that's so ancient it has those miniature, individual jukeboxes (blaring vintage ranchera hits) sitting right on the bar... and they don't even know how cool that is!

And though LA's beach communities are packed with fun 'n' sun, there's a dark side, too. In 1935, movie comedienne Thelma Todd, known as "The Ice Cream Blonde" met an with an untimely — and rather suspicious — death by asphyxiation in the garage above her club, **Thelma Todd's Roadside Café** (no longer standing) on Pacific Coast Highway in Malibu. The coroner ruled it a suicide, but those in the know insisted it was a hit ordered by the infamous Bugsy Seigel, who apparently thought Todd knew too much about his numbers racket and casino on the private second floor of her café. During the same time period, Seigel and his Murder, Inc. partners Meyer Lansky and Lucky Luciano were also responsible for Santa Monica Bay's "floating casinos" (luxury yachts serving up liquor, ultra-high stakes card games, slot machines and roulette wheels — giving new meaning to the term 'floating crap game!') anchored a mile or so off the beach in Santa Monica Bay. Many people think this is just an urban legend, but it's true, down to the movie star clientele and the champagne-drenched dinghies that used to ferry the glitterati back and forth. This kind of stuff, of course, doesn't exist any more... but if you aren't a beach-type person and you're stuck on the West Side, then here's what you do: visit **The Apple Pan** (10801 West Pico Blvd., Westwood). Opened in 1947, famous for its delicious pies and Hickory Burgers. Sit at the counter and the crazed, paper-hat-wearing cooks serve you (and five other people) simultaneously, even pouring ketchup on your fries! The pies are made fresh daily, and one heavenly mouthful is like taking a bite out of LA history.

TRIPPING THROUGH LAUREL CANYON
(Not that kind of tripping)
Decadent Lifestyles of the Rich, Famous and (for the most part) Dead
Libby Molyneaux and Joe Hill

Only a few minutes from the Sunset Strip is **Laurel Canyon**, the famous refuge favored more by boho musicians, writers and porn stars rather than the glamorous set who flock to the ritzier canyons to the west. Today, it's home to a gaggle of sitcom actors who drive Ford Explorers, but not so long ago Laurel Canyon was like a freaky Shangri-La. This is an LA history tour tailored to people who, with just a bit of imagination, want to peek in and imagine what inspired Joni Mitchell, Jim Morrison, and John Holmes to call it home. While many of the sights are part of popular LA lore, elements of its wild past can still discovered with a little sniffing. And a lot of sniffing has gone on in Laurel Canyon.

The following route was designed to explore by bicycle. Or you can walk it in sections. Few souls are seen peddling around here, so you may even get cheers of encouragement from neighbors. (And who knows, maybe Ice-T, who lives up here, will invite you in for a glass of his eponymous beverage.) Yes, parts of it are excruciatingly steep and evil, but not only will you be rewarded with some of the most stupendous views of LA (some of which are not accessible by car), but you can feel just like Pamela and Jim as you trudge the hilly terrain, smell the eucalyptus and get the same dizzy sensation on the majestic overlooks. (If you must drive, at least listen to some John Mayall/Doors tapes, and stop and get out as much as possible.)

1. A good starting point is the **Canyon Country Store** (2108 Laurel Canyon Blvd.), with its flowery sign still day-glo-ing. Harry Houdini, who had quite a spread up the street, never bought a six-pack here, but you can usually count on seeing some luminary stocking up on better-quality munchies.

2. That's **Jim Morrison's house** (now rebuilt) on Rothdell Trail, next to the cleaners. Rumor has it he may have done a drug in these parts.

3. View time! Head up (and up and up) Kirkwood Drive. At the top, take a very sharp left on Grand View Drive (level ground!) then take a quick, very sharp right on Colecrest Drive. It's steep again for a bit; then turn right to stay on Colecrest and it's a very steep 50 feet until you have a 270-degree view that sweeps **Laurel Canyon**, all the way to the familiar sights of Hollywood and downtown, including the **Griffith Park Observatory**, the **Hollywood sign**, and the **Capitol Records Building**. It's a knockout.

4. Continue to the top of Colecrest Drive (you're almost there already). You'll pass over a driveway to get to Blue

Heights Drive; look down and through the bushes to see the **Big Blue Whale**, a.k.a. the Pacific Design Center, while going downhill. Blue Heights spits you out on Sunset Plaza Drive: turn right, after a gradual uphill and a few twists it turns into Appian Way. Take a break at the former home of **Carole King** (8815 Appian Way). In the late '60s, she sat in the house's bay window for the cover of *Tapestry*.

5. Next, fly down Lookout (look out!) Mountain Avenue. (It's dangerous and skinny — did we mention bicyclists should wear a helmet?) Turn left at Wonderland Elementary School (uphill again!). It's a steep climb. **Alice Cooper**, **Keith Moon**, **John Densmore**, **David Crosby**, and **John Mayall** lived on this street. At the top, it bends right, then left, and turns into a dirt road. It makes a loop, full of ruts... but at least it's flat! This secret (until now) gem of a view boasts incredible (and incredibly quiet) southward views of Beverly Hills to the ocean (and Catalina when the fog is low). As an added bonus, you can peek down into people's backyards and swimming pools, and see straight down Doheny.

6. Now descend back down Wonderland Avenue. Well-endowed porn star **John Holmes** was accused (and acquitted) of murdering five people in a drug-related incident at 8763 Wonderland Avenue in '81.

7. Take a sharp left and go up Wonderland Park Avenue. Right on Greenvalley Road; left on Crest View Drive; left on Skyline Drive to Mulholland Drive and head right (east). Try to pick out the house on Mulholland where **Danny Sugarman** (former Doors associate who co-wrote "No One Here Gets Out Alive") flew his car off the road and onto a house after a night of alcohol and Quaaludes at the Rainbow Room on the Strip. The car landed right side up on the flat roof of somebody's house, caving it in; Danny and his girlfriend left the car in the living room and walked to his house on

Wonderland to do speedballs. Happily (and surprisingly), Danny's still alive.

8. Continue on Mulholland through the light at Laurel Canyon Boulevard. Almost immediately, make a right on Woodrow Wilson Drive. This shady, mostly flat, bucolic road has more than its share of grisly history. At 8000 Woodrow Wilson, actress **Inger Stevens** overdosed in 1970 at age 35 (she played Katy on mid-'60s sitcom, *The Farmer's Daughter*). At 7944, another little-known starlet **Gia Scala** drank and pilled herself to death in 1972 at age 38. And nearby at 7357, another Hollywood dreamer you've probably never heard of, **Aleta Alexander**, took a rifle to herself. At the age of 28, she was having trouble getting roles and had found out her more successful husband, actor **Ross Alexander**, was cheating on her. He did the same with that very rifle about a year later. 6969 is the address where character actor **Frank Christi** was shot in a drug-ambush in his carport.

9. Double back a little on Woodrow Wilson and turn right (north) on Passmore Drive; right on Oakshire Drive; and left on Oak Glen Drive. At 3429 Oak Glen is the house where Oakland Raider/actor **John Matusak** croaked after drugs attacked his heart in 1989.

10. Enough death already. Wind back to Woodrow Wilson, go right (west) a little and turn left on Montcalm (south) and left on Pyramid Place to get to Mulholland. Across the street is the entrance to **Runyon Canyon**. Take the dirt path up and down to one of the many lookout spots where you have the City of Angels at your feet. If it's a smoggy day, you can just make out an **Angelyne** billboard a little west of the Capitol Records building. There's something special about being in this untamed, wild park knowing that you're 1,200 feet above an entirely different sort of untamed, wild place.

11. Head back (west) on Mulholland. Turn left on Woodrow Wilson, then left (south) on Woodstock Road, and right on Willow Glen Road, which takes you down to Laurel Canyon Boulevard. On the southeast corner are the sprawling remains of the **Harry Houdini** estate. It was only the widow Houdini who actually called the rambling hillside manor home, but her Halloween séances to bring back Harry's spirit are legendary. After a devastating fire, the only structural remains are the stone fireplaces and staircases, along with a dilapidated servants' quarters. We recommend you keep your distance at night: creepy crawlies of the human persuasion are regularly seen coming and going. During the day, it's easy to connect the dots and imagine the elegant parties in the early 1900s. The vacant lot at Lookout Mountain and Laurel Canyon Boulevard is where **Frank Zappa** lived from '66-'68. Just up at 2451 Laurel Canyon Boulevard is the haunted mansion where the **Red Hot Chili Peppers** recorded "Bloodsugar sexmagic". Members of **Love and Rockets** lived here until a fire damaged the inside in '96.

12. Go up Lookout Mountain a little. Below Wonderland Avenue Elementary School is **Joni Mitchell**'s former home where she lived during her "Ladies of the Canyon" and "Clouds" period. Picture Joni looking out the kitchen window and sketching the cover drawing for "Ladies of the Canyon". Her live-in lover at the time, **Graham Nash**, wrote "Our House" about this very, very, very fine house. Do not disturb the two cats in the yard.

P.S. Remember: The Thomas Bros. are an LA explorer's best friends. Get one of their guides before launching on this worthwhile expedition. For further reading, check out "Wonderland Avenue" by Danny Sugarman; Ken Schessler's "This Is Hollywood"; and "The LA Musical History Tour" by Art Fein.

PASADENA and BEYOND
Mary Herczog

Way up here in the real hills, in the other Valley (San Gabriel, thank you very much), we, the residents of Altadena and Pasadena, have to constantly explain to the geographically impaired that we are not off the face of the earth. Actually, we are a mere twenty minutes away from Hollywood, by freeway. And frankly, everything in Los Angeles is at least twenty minutes away from everything else, not to mention freeway accessible. Here you can get away from some of the crowds, see much more of the truly lovely architecture that originally characterized LA (but in most of the rest of the city has been torn down in favor of mini-malls), gawk at the mountains, and even walk around... a rare occurrence in most of the greater Los Angeles area.

ALTADENA

Since it's neither a city nor a neighborhood of a city, Altadena suffers from a serious identity crisis. But check this out; the North Hollywood bank robbers (the Kevlar-clad, Uzi-toting guys who went down in a haze of bullets and glory in early 1997) were Altadena residents, as was motorist **Rodney King**. We don't have crime - we just export it to other parts of the city. But we do have **Jackie Robinson**'s alma mater. Yes, the first black major league ballplayer went to **Muir High School** (1905 Lincoln Ave.).

Drive north on Lincoln into the hills area called the La Vina development. This was the site of the La Vina Sanitarium. In 1931, **Winnie Ruth Judd** was picked up for questioning after someone noticed the trunk she had with her on the train to LA smelled - it was full of hacked-up bodies (those of her ex-roommates). Winnie escaped from police questioning and walked twenty miles to hide out at the sanitarium (where she had once been a patient) before giving herself up.

Go back down Lincoln to Altadena Dr. and turn left (heading east). As the houses get nicer, you might suddenly think you are in Beverly Hills - particularly if you watch reruns of the classic 1990s' soap opera, **Beverly Hills, 90210**. You'd be right; much of the show's exteriors were filmed here and in Pasadena. That's Brandon and Brenda Walsh's house on the left, at 1675.

If you feel like a hike, drive up to **Cheney Trail** (off Loma Alta, between Lincoln and Fair Oaks). Park at the top, and hike down to the waterfall or campgrounds. You can also try **Eaton Canyon**, just off Altadena Dr. to the west. For those who prefer to take their exercise in a different way, have a stroll in the **Mountain View Cemetery** (2400 N. Fair Oaks Ave, 626-794-7133). Thanks to the dreaded Hubert Eaton (the man who brought us Forest Lawn and the modern concept of "memorial parks" with flat, flush-to-the-ground headstones), cemeteries — particularly out here, where Eaton flourished — have lost a lot of their ambiance. Mountain View still has plenty of upright headstones, which are growing very rare. Even with the palm trees, this is everything a good, eerie cemetery should be... with a little extra Raymond Chandler atmosphere.

Food and Drink

Coffee Gallery (2029 Lake, 626-398-7917, www.coffee gallery.com) This cozy java joint is home to **Coffee Gallery Backstage**, a performance space designed to look like a Central American warehouse. It hosts a variety of musical acts ranging from folkies, swing combos and world music to the singing, joking cowboy Sourdough Slim. Over the years it's become quite a regular scene, which obviously means gossip and infighting as much as the official entertainment. The cover varies, but expect to pay $15-20.

Fox's (2352 N. Lake, 626-797-9430) A tiny hole-in-the-wall local tradition with a coffeehouse (serving fine iced mochas) in the back. Expect long weekend breakfast lines: their biscuits and cream gravy are to die for. Check out the scary stuffed foxes on the walls.

Dutch Oven Bakery (2281 N. Lake, 626-794-3555) Friendly, family-run business with huge tasty muffins, cake made from scratch, and fresh bread. The owner often waits on customers and everyone who works here will chat about everything from computers to Bill Clinton's sex life.

Patticakes (1900 N. Allen, 626-794-1128) An expensive chi-chi bakery, but with exceptional high-rent muffins and pastries. Go ahead, blow your budget.

Little **Middle Eastern** places, from cafes to grocery stores, will be found if you drive around on both Allen (south of Patticakes) and east and west on Washington (using Allen as the center). Each is totally different and worth taste-testing. (The grocery story on Allen is particularly fun; try the fresh meat and cheese-topped breads delivered every morning.)

Stores

Mitchell Books (1395 E. Washington Blvd., 626-798-4438) is run by a massive, tattooed, biker-type guy who is an odd mix of reactionary and liberal (doesn't that spell "libertarian?"). Mitchell Books has every crime/mystery novel you can think of — and many you didn't know existed. The owner is incredibly chatty; he talks knowledgeably about politics (on both a global and local scale) and just about anything else you can imagine. He also makes trustworthy book recommendations... he knows his stuff.

PASADENA

Best known for floral parade floats on New Year's Day, Pasadena is usually hidden the rest of the time - because originally, it was Old Money, and that's the way Old Money likes it. It's becoming more high profile of late, thanks to a renovation of **Old Town Pasadena**, the stretch of Colorado Blvd. usually seen as part of The Parade. (Don't forget the anti-Rose Parade, the **Doo-Dah Parade**, which takes place Thanksgiving Day weekend and features such entries as the Synchronized Briefcase Drill Team. It's an ode to the eccentric.) The crumbling 1920s office buildings had fallen into slum-like disrepair, and a few years ago quite a lot of money was sunk into renovating and cleaning up the place. Unfortunately, upscale chain stores (**Urban Outfitters, J. Crew, Victoria's Secret**, and now even **Tiffany**) came in, pushing out most of the mom-and-pop independent stores and turning the place into a (very pretty) outdoor mall. And attracting crowds; if you really like the concept of personal space, skip this area on a Friday or Saturday night. However, it is a nice place to hang out on an un-crowded night. Plus, the **Adult Bookstore** is still holding their ground; bless their hearts, they took their grimy, trench coat-like exterior and redid it in yuppie glass and neon to blend in with their newly upscale neighbors. Clients remain of the trench-coat sort, though, so this is for sleazy fun only.

On Fair Oaks, just south of Green (which is parallel to Colorado, on the south), look up at the side of the building on the west and read a portion of these words: "**Lawrence, picking up his fork.**" Originally, it read, "'My people are the people of the desert,' said T. E. Lawrence, picking up his fork." The Whittier earthquake badly damaged this old building, and some bricks with most of the words fell off, so it started at "said T. E. Lawrence" for many years. Recently, a paint job obscured even more of it, further increasing its cryptic nature.

The **Castle Green Hotel** (www.castelgreen.com) is a residence hotel that covers nearly a block between Raymond and Fair Oaks, on Green St. It's a gorgeous, huge old Gothic number and one can't help but think the people who live there are very lucky. The following are other Old Town establishments worth visiting: **Equator Coffee House** (22 Mills Pl., 626-564-8656) is a funky, airy place with not only a huge variety of coffee drinks, but also some righteous smoothies (and flavored hot chocolate with flavored whip cream!) which stood in as the "gay coffeehouse" on "Beverly Hills, 90210". Ignore the Starbucks across the street (Equator is actually hidden in an alley off Colorado) and come to the real McCoy. "90210" buffs can also go to the **Peach Pit** (45 S. Fair Oaks), which is really **Ruby's Diner** — the exterior, then the venerable Rose City Café — was used in the show. See actual movies, as opposed to movie locations, at the **Academy**

Theaters (1003 E Colorado Blvd., 626-229-9400), an inexpensive, six-screen, "last chance" venue specializing in (sometimes the more obscure) art house flicks, though with the occasional Hollywood blockbuster. It has had a bit of a facelift since its rather seedy days.

Hooked on **Zankou Chicken**? They have a branch here, hooray! (1296 E Colorado Blvd., 626-405-1502; www.zankouchicken.com.)

Kuala Lampur (69 W. Green St.) may be your only chance to try Malaysian food, outside of Malaysia, that is. Think Thai, only different.

Hot Hot Hot (130 N. Fair Oaks at CJ's Gourmet) Hot sauces, hot peppers, hot oils — really, anything that can be made with chilies. Out You Devil hot sauce, Vampire's Kiss hot sauce, all kinds of sauces you never knew about but burn the roof of your mouth. Some of the labels on the sauces are so hilarious, you don't care if they taste good.

Soda Jerks (219 S. Fair Oaks, 626-583-8031) is actually just a little south of Old Town, but is an airy, old-fashioned-looking (maybe with genuine fixtures) soda fountain, serving the fabulous **Fosselman's ice cream**. Not as good as **Fair Oaks Soda Fountain** in S. Pasadena, and a little more expensive, but much, much better than going to a prefab place. They also serve food.

Flea Markets

Pasadena is home to the two best flea markets in Southern California. The first is at **Pasadena City College** (1570 E. Colorado Blvd; www.pasadena.edu/fleamarket). Free on the first Sunday of the month. It's a good size; big, but not so big you can't cover the whole ground. Record nerds will find nirvana (or Nirvana) at the Record Swap portion, where vinyl still rules. The Aes-Nihil gang (including former Germs drummer, Don Bolles) can often be found holding court in this section, and selling serial killer, Manson-related, Church of Satan, and other underground pop culture books, along with their massive collection of naughty/subversive videos (we recommend the infamous Go-Go's porno tape).

The second Sunday of the month hosts the mammoth **Rose Bowl Swap Meet** (1001 Rose Bowl Dr; www.rosebowl stadium.com/RoseBowl_flea-market). It's the mother of all swap meets, covering acres of ground, including genuine antique dealers, piles of junk, and new tacky items; just when you think you've seen it all you find another football field full of stuff. There is an admission fee: up to $10; early birds get a discount, not to mention the best pickings.

Museums

No mention of Pasadena can neglect the **Norton Simon Museum** (411 W. Colorado Blvd., 626-449-6840; www.norton simon.org), a world-class collection mostly devoted to Impressionists and their contemporaries. But far cooler is the **Huntington Library Art Collections and Botanical Gardens** (1151 Oxford Rd., San Marino, 626-405-2141; www.hunting ton.org). Formerly the vast estate of a robber baron, like the Getty family after him, he turned his art collection and home into a museum. The grounds are huge and varied; one moment you are walking on English estate-type grounds, complete with rolling lawns, large trees, and the odd sculpture; the next minute you are in a tropical jungle, or a desert filled with cactus and other succulents. There's a Japanese garden with a teahouse, babbling brook, and Half Moon Bridge. There's a rose garden. A Shakespeare garden. And on (and on) it goes. The library itself has a Guttenberg Bible on display, among many other treasures. And the art museum, housed in Huntington's own former residence, has still more fabulous items, including Gainsborough's "Blue Boy" and the matching painting known as "Pinky." Pay them a visit, but once you've marveled at their icon status, look at the same wall Blue Boy is on, all the way to the right. See the painting of a dark-haired girl in the large hat; chin perched in hand, looking coyly at you? She's the famous Emma Hamilton, for whom British Naval hero Lord Nelson endured so much scandal (they were both married at the time of their lengthy affair). When you look at this portrait, you suddenly understand what all the fuss is about. (Now go rent *That Hamilton Woman* and see how they superimposed Vivian Leigh's face onto a copy of this same portrait.) Before you go to the Huntington, make a reservation at their **Rose Garden Tea Room**; at around $19.95 for an all-you-can eat buffet (including tasty finger sandwiches and strawberries with creme fraiche), it's the best afternoon tea in the city; reservations are suggested. Afterwards, walk off the many calories by exploring the grounds... or just nap under a tree. Admission : $15 for adults, $12 for seniors, $10 for students 12-18 years old, or full-time student with ID, $5 for ages 5 to 11, and free for under 5; the first Thursday of the month, admission is free. Equally as cool, and located in the heart of Pasadena, the **Pasadena Museum of California Art** (490 East Union Street, 626-568-3665, www.pmcaonline.org, free on Fridays) houses several artists' work at a time. Past exhibits have included cutting-edge symbolists Mark Ryden and Gary Baseman, along with plein-air California Impressionists and sculptors. The parking garage, with its pop art murals, is a work of fun, glowing art.

The Bunny Museum (1933 Jefferson Dr., 626-798-8848, www.thebunnymuseum.com) We know that, left to their own devices, rabbits, er, multiply, and so perhaps that explains the 20,000 — and growing — bunny-related objets d'art at this wacky and adorable collection. Located in a private home, it's a remarkable illustration of mania in action, complete with canonization (Largest in the World) by the Guinness Book of World Records. Stuffed bunnies, china bunnies, comic bunnies, lifelike bunnies, Rose Parade float bunnies... if you think it's all just Peter Cottontail and Bugs and Beanie Babies, you are so, so wrong. If you can stand the cute — oh, don't make us say it — hop on over. Open 365 days a year, by appointment only, call for reservations.

Stores

Vroman's Books (695 E. Colorado Blvd., 626-449-5320; www.vromansbookstore.com) Around since 1930, Vroman's is big and well-stocked. Book savvy, helpful staff. There is also a better-than-average magazine stand outside, heavy on the literary journals. Take your new reading matters into **Zoli's**, the cushy, mildly Victorian Gothic-looking cafe with some terrific (if pricey) desserts and some savory munchies, washed down with a "frozen hot chocolate" frothy drink that's like drinking a candy bar.

Cliff's Books (630 E. Colorado, 626-449-9541) A used bookstore that is, quite honestly, a little overpriced and a bit attitudinal. But they are huge (as opposed to their more kind-hearted and pleasant - but considerably smaller - competitors across the street; pay them a visit at the same time). Open until midnight every night.

Aaardvark's Odd Ark (1253 E. Colorado, 626-583-9109) A chain vintage shop - they probably snatch all the good stuff from the real thrift store across the street (but just in case, go by there as well). Well-stocked, but not terribly cheap. Still, they have tons of used Levis, Army pants, racks and racks of dresses and whatnot. And they aren't nearly as rude or expensive as the branch on Melrose Avenue in Hollywood.

Poobah Record Shop (1101 E. Walnut., 626-449-3359; www.poobah.com) Located in an old house in a non-business district part of Pasadena, this place is crammed with new and used CDs, some vinyl, imports and a staff that breathes music.

Restaurants

Burger Continental (535 S. Lake Ave., 626-792-6634, www.burgercontinental.com) Now wait; this is not, repeat, not a burger joint. In fact, the worst thing anyone can do is order a burger at Burger Continental. Regulars will laugh at you. You will be revealed as a tourist. Because this is one of the best Middle Eastern restaurants around. Small sums of money get you enormous plates of food. Not just the usual kebobs and shawarma, but also garlic buttery chicken, chicken stuffed with spinach and feta and pine nuts, vegetarian specialties, and on and on. The menu is huger than huge, and if that's not enough, there is a whiteboard with the day's specials; a dozen or more combination plates, each with an adjective assuring it is "delicious!" "outstanding!" "delectable!" All dinners come with hummus, salad bar, stuffed grape leaves, and more. You will almost certainly end up with enough for lunch the next day, making the medium-priced meals even more of a bargain. Often, the owner wanders the line (you order at a window and sit in a charming patio where a band plays and a bellydancer shakes), giving discounts to everyone just for the hell of it ("First time here? Ten percent off!"). It's a wacky place and will make both veggies and carnivores happy. Go early and often.

La Luna Negra (44 W. Green St., 626-844-4331, www.lalunanegra.qpg.com) is a low-key romantic Spanish spot, with a large menu, including several varieties of paella and dozens of tapas options.

Pie 'n' Burger (913 E. California Blvd., 626-795-1123, www.pienburger.com) Now here, you order the burger. This is where you go when you want the real thing: big, juicy, slathered in goopy stuff, made on a grill as you sit at a low Formica counter. Burger Heaven. The pies (and homemade cakes) aren't bad either, but skip the shakes.

Sushi of Naples (735 E. Green St., 626-578-1123, www.sushiofnaples.com) Better than average sushi, predictably fresh and tender. Call first and go only if they are still offering their Happy Hour; most of each evening they sell their sushi half-price, which makes it very affordable.

The Hat (491 N. Lake, 626-449-1844, www.thehat.com) A local food critic once made the distinction between good pastrami and bad pastrami: the former is the hearty stuff you get at a classic New York deli, the latter is the French dip, greasy-style kind; you can feel your arteries harden even as your taste buds dance in glee. And The Hat, everyone agrees, is the best of Bad Pastrami.

Tibet Nepal House (36 E. Holly St., 626-585-9955; www.tibetnepalhouse.com) is a shock these days, since it's such an oddball compared to the sleek n' pretty image of Pasadena; can the chainstore set really appreciate authentic Tibetan food? No matter; you certainly can, especially during their lunch buffet ($6.95, all you can eat). If you come at dinner, be sure to try the Momo dumplings. Leave time for shopping in the attached store, full of all those Nepal geegaws (clothes are overpriced, but there can be some good jewelry and religious article deals) so beloved by the yoga crowd.

SOUTH PASADENA

It is indeed south of Pasadena and more small town in feeling. David Lynch staple **Jack Nance** (star of *Eraserhead*) got into a fight at the **Winchell's Donuts** at 438 Fair Oaks, and died from his injuries some days later at his home across the street at 509 Fair Oaks.

Fair Oaks Pharmacy and Soda Fountain (1526 Mission St., 626-799-1414) In operation since the '20s, but recently renovated with fixtures from a Midwestern turn-of-the-century pharmacy/soda fountain; the owner's condition for sale was that it be used in a working pharmacy. So now there's a hammered tin ceiling, gorgeous wood and beveled glass cabinets, plus a marble-topped soda fountain counter. The ice cream is perfect; they use **Fosselman's**, a local tradition since 1913. When you taste it, you will know why. Caution: they use over a pint of ice cream in their shakes, which is more than any one person needs to consume at a sitting. Split one.

Rialto Theatre (1023 Fair Oaks, 626-388-2122) One of the last great old movie palaces, a little shabby despite some renovations. Check out the demon with red glowing eyes at the top of the proscenium. Best of all, they show art house movies; no Spielberg here. Combine this with some ice cream at the Fair Oaks Pharmacy just up the street, and you'll be transported to a different era.

The Bookhouse (1026 Fair Oaks Ave., 626-799-0756) A very well-stocked used bookstore with a friendly book-aware staff, set inside a sweet Craftsman-style old house.

Senor Fish (618 Mission, 626-403-0145) Foodie and ethnic food fans know this little stand is the place to go for fish tacos.

SIERRA MADRE

This is a genuine small town plunked down in the middle of the big city. It's got a main street lined with stores of varying interest — a great coffeeshop, coupla good restaurants, a few antique stores — and it may look oddly familiar. That's because this stood in for the small town in *Invasion of the Body Snatchers*. Wander around and feel like a pod person... just kidding. It's very pretty and peaceful. The mountains are right there with several good hiking trails; ask around for directions to the different access roads. Afterwards, have a bite at the **Corfu Cafe** (48 W. Sierra Madre Blvd., 626-355-5993). This is a good choice for a cheap breakfast or lunch; dinner is slightly more pricey but probably delicious. Service is slow, so be in the mood to dawdle. Lunch brings huge salads and sandwiches, with nothing over $9. Try the large Greek Salad, or the Brie Chicken sandwich (Brie and chicken on a French roll, with bacon and red onions, all pressed down like a Cuban sandwich. It's sooo fattening. It's so delicious.)

MONTERY PARK and ALHAMBRA

These two communities lie a bit south of South Pasadena, between ten and twenty minutes' drive. If you like Chinese food, make the trip. *This cannot be urged strongly enough.* Forget Chinatown in downtown LA; this is the Chinese community in the LA area, and is rapidly becoming Little Hong Kong. There are dozens of Chinese restaurants down here varying in cuisine, price, and quality. Just drive and pick one out (the huge palace-like restaurants are usually safe bets), but here are two to keep an eye out for. **Ocean Star Restaurant** (112 N. Chandler Ave., Montery Park, 626-281-5288) serves incredibly fresh seafood plucked from the tank. The large eatery also does *major* dim sum. Dumpling fans will be more than happy at **Dumpling House** (5612 Rosemead Blvd, 626-309-9918).

Fosselman's Ice Cream Parlor (1824 W. Main, Alhambra, 626-282-6533) As mentioned, this family business started making ice cream in 1913 - plenty long enough to get it oh so right. It's incredible stuff: you will never bother with Haagen-Daaz again. Several Pasadena places serve Fosselman's, but not only is it cheaper at the source, it's just fun to go to a real (if tiny) ice cream parlor again. After eating your fill of dim sum, come here and explode.

VALLEY of the MALLS
The San Fernando Valley
Iris Berry

It doesn't matter where you are in the San Fernando Valley, if you throw a rock you're sure to hit a Mall. Born and raised a Valley Girl, I can attest to that. Hey, I happen to love the mall, it's air-conditioned, tons of great and crappy food from all walks of life, I get great reception on my cell phone and "like, OHMYGAWD!" there's always a sale going on. But more than malls, the San Fernando Valley has really amazing vintage stores with great prices and some truly unique restaurants. It's also been the setting for many historic and countercultural happenings that have reverberated throughout the world and hey... if the Valley is good enough for Bob Hope, Johnny Carson, Charles Manson, and Moon Unit Zappa, well then, it's good enough for me!

MALLS

GLENDALE GALLERIA (50 W. Broadway, Glendale, 818-240-9481, www.glendalegalleria.com) Rumor has it that Lux and Ivy of The Cramps have been spotted here (on more than one occasion) visiting the food court at ten in the morning. What I want to know is: what were they doing here? Make sure you take a compass with you, this place is huge. There's an **Apple Store** for your computin' needs, an awesome **Sephora** for beauty product junkies, and check out **Forever 21** for bargain Britney Spears-type fashions.

SHERMAN OAKS GALLERIA (15303 Ventura Blvd., Sherman Oaks, 818-382-4100, www.shermanoaks galleria.com) put on the map in 1982 by Moon Unit Zappa's hit song, "Valley Girl." Recently remodeled, nipped, tucked and lifted... super fabulous!

FASHION SQUARE SHERMAN OAKS (14006 Riverside Dr., Sherman Oaks, 818-783-0550, www.fashion squareshermanoaks.com) The kinder, gentler mall, as I like to call it. Skylights, split-level food court, and convenient, stress-free roof parking. Weekends a piano player takes requests. Quite the pick-up scene for the over-65 set.

NORTHRIDGE FASHION CENTER (9301 Tampa Ave., Northridge, 818-885-9700, www.northridgefashion center.com) Fully restored after being demolished by the '94 Northridge quake. It's back and more dazzling than ever.

WESTFIELD SHOPPINGTOWN PROMENADE (6100 Topanga Canyon Blvd., Woodland Hills, 818-884-7090, shoppingtown.com) Recently remodeled high-tech theatres with those really comfy seats that move and adjust and recline. Connected to a fancy-shmancy food court.

WESTFIELD SHOPPINGTOWN TOPANGA (6600 Topanga Canyon Blvd., Canoga Park, 818-594-8740, www.shoppingtown.com) Site of one of my first mall experiences as a child. Great food court with a real train ride for the young 'uns.

THE COMMONS AT CALABASAS (4799 Common Way, Calabasas, 818-222-3444) The Commons is an extremely pretty and serene outdoor mall with piped-in music and waterfalls, surrounded by picturesque green rolling hills. A nice place to shop as long as you don't mind five-year-olds on cell phones and sixteen–year-olds driving brand new Mercedes Benz SUVs.

THE STUDIOS

NBC STUDIOS (3000 W. Alameda Ave., Burbank, 818-840-3538, www.nbc.com) NBC Studios is where the term "Beautiful Downtown Burbank" was coined during the filming of "Laugh-in." NBC is also the place to see Jay Leno taping live. There's a 70-minute tour that takes you behind the scenes of "The Tonight Show": wardrobe, makeup, set construction, special effects, and sound effects departments. Oh boy!

WALT DISNEY STUDIOS (500 S. Buena Vista St., Burbank, 818-560-1000, www.disney.go.com) This studio offers nothing in the way of rides because it's not Disneyland; it's a *studio*, although at one time, they were going to build Disneyland right across the street. Then they realized they needed more space and bought 200 acres in Anaheim instead. The studio does offer a hint of Disney in its architecture: holding up the House of Mouse are none other than the Seven Dwarves themselves. Not bad for a bunch of guys who've been around since 1937. Rumor has it that if you listen closely, you can actually hear the seven helpers whistling (while they work).

WARNER BROTHERS STUDIOS TOUR (4000 Warner Blvd., Burbank, 818-954-1744, www.warnerbros.com/vip_tours). Offering a two-hour VIP tour that visits actual working areas and soundstages. Tours conducted by reservation only. Warner Brothers also has live tapings of shows. For tickets and information call Audiences Unlimited, 818-753-3470.

UNIVERSAL STUDIOS TOUR (100 Universal City Plaza, Universal City, 1-800-UNIVERSAL, www.universal studios.com) A full day of rides, movie-making, star and star-impersonator gazing, as well as Hollywood-induced earthquakes, fires, dinosaur and shark attacks. Visit old sets, too, like the *Psycho* house. Growing up with three older brothers who were constant troublemakers, this is one more place that my family almost got thrown out of. While on the set of "The Munsters" my brother Don kept trying to set Spot (the Munster's "family dragon") free. We were warned (and as usual, shamed) in front of the whole tour!

UNIVERSAL AMPHITHEATRE (100 Universal City Plaza, Universal City, 818-777-1000) a great place to see concerts, comedians and political speakers.

UNIVERSAL CITY WALK (3900 Lankershim Blvd., Universal City, 818-622-9841, www.citywalk.com) Imagine a perfect LA? City Walk has attempted to replicate the best places in Tinsel Town and put them all in one spot. The only thing missing is Dodger Stadium... but I'm sure they're making plans. There's a multi-screen cinema, souvenir shops, a couple of rock clubs (with live music), good eats (both restaurants and snack stands), huge video screens, and street performers. Around Christmas, they make a big outdoor ice-skating rink and rent skates. Ample parking, too.

CBS STUDIOS CENTER (CBS Studio Center, 4024 Radford Ave., Studio City, 818-655-5000, www.cbs.com) One of the smaller, more homey studios... originally owned by Mack Sennett (of *Keystone Cops* fame) in the 1920s, giving the city its name, "Studio City." Among the many TV shows that have been filmed here are "Gilligan's Island" and "Hawaii Five O"... Yes, the ocean shots must have been edited in, but up until the mid '80s one could actually find the Lagoon from "Gilligan's Island" in the back part of the studios. "Three-hour tour," my ass! They were in the Valley!

FOOD

THE CASTAWAYS (1250 Harvard Road, Burbank, 818-848-6691) A big banquet-type restaurant on a hill. Wherever you sit, there's an amazing view of the San Fernando Valley and the Los Angeles skyline. Too bad the food and the service (at least in the main dining room) suck! I've tried so many times to like this place because the view is so goddamn incredible! So here's what I figured out: if you sit on the outdoor patio, around one of the fire pits with the view of the city at your feet, preferably at sundown, sip cocktails, order dinner off the moderately-priced bar menu, and just stay out of the main dining room, *no matter what*, a night at the Castaways can be fabulous.

THE SMOKE HOUSE (4420 Lakeside Drive, Burbank, 818-845-3733, smokehouserestaurant.net) A Burbank staple for years, the Smoke House is conveniently located right across the street from the Warner Brothers Studios lot, and known for being a historic neighborhood hang to the stars. Also known for its prime rib, painfully good garlic bread, and Sunday brunches. The Smoke House often appeared in episodes of "The Larry Sanders Show" and countless episodes of "Columbo."

TOKYO DELVES SUSHI BAR (5239 Lankershim Blvd., N. Hollywood, 818-766-3868, www.delve-sushi bar.com) One of the wildest restaurants in town! So wild that they have a disclaimer hanging at the front door that reads, "If you stand on the chairs or the tables, we don't take responsibility or liability for anything that happens!" Loud music, fun, crazy people (including staff as well as patrons), reasonably priced sushi.

JERRY'S FAMOUS 24 HOUR DELICATESSEN (12655 Ventura Blvd., Studio City, 818-980-4245, www.jerrys deli.com) A menu that offers over 600 dishes, including huge sandwiches, awesome kosher pickles, breakfasts, and mega-yummy fries. And no, it's not named after Jerry Seinfeld, although he is known to frequent the place so much that he even has his own table.

DR. HOGLEY WOGLEY'S TEXAS TYLER BBQ (8136 Sepulveda Blvd., Van Nuys, 818-782-2480) For some, Dr. Hogley Wogley's is the *only* reason to come to the San Fernando Valley. Serving amazing BBQ for over 30 years.

THE QUEEN MARY (12449 Ventura Blvd., Studio City, 818-506-5619) giving us female impersonator shows for 40 years straight... or, rather, for the last forty years. The building was originally bought from May West, go figure!

SPORTSMENS LODGE (4234 Coldwater Canyon, Studio City, 818-755-5000, sportsmens lodge.com) Imagine the Sunday all-you-can-eat buffet, surrounded by exotic gardens and a pond with real swans swimming by, trying to decide whether you want more crab legs or more lobster... What a dilemma!

VITELLO'S (4349 Tujunga Ave., Studio City, 818-769-0905, www.vitellos.com) Now, we all know about this place because of a famous celebrity murder mystery — can you say "Baretta"? But the food is really good, too.

AROMA CAFE (4360 Tujunga Ave., Studio City, 818-508-6505) Great neighborhood coffeehouse and eatery. Connected to a bookstore called "Portrait Of A Book Store" offering great books, gifts, and vintage toys for kiddies. Outdoor seating. Waterfalls, dogs and sitcom actors, oh my!

COBALT CAFE (22047 Sherman Way, Canoga Park, 818-348-3789, www.cobaltcafe.com) Large, comfortable punk rock coffeehouse showcasing under-age hardcore bands and spoken word.

THE INN OF THE SEVENTH RAY (128 Old Topanga Canyon Rd., Topanga, 310-455-1311, www.innofthe seventhray.com) Romantic, gourmet natural food, creekside dining, no processed sugars on the premises. They've been catering to vegetarians, vegans and wheat-free eaters since the '70s. Lots of people get married here.

FOLLOW YOUR HEART (21825 Sherman Way, Canoga Park, 818-348-3240, followyour heart.com) Healthfood market and restaurant. Visiting this place is like taking a walk into the 1970s... the restaurant offers meatless clubs and Reubens. Whatever kind of diet you're on, they can cater to it.

SAGEBRUSH CANTINA (23527 Calabasas Road, Calabasas, 818-222-6062, sagebrush cantina.com) The Sagebrush has a reputation as being a "wild" Valley hang. Huge outdoor patio, widescreen TVs for sports events. Full bar, Mexican food, burgers, seafood, salads, and desserts. Every Sunday, motorcyclists from all over mix with families, tourists, strippers, and locals, becoming a regular modern-day saloon and the breeding ground for the "Jewish American Biker." Big fun!

STORES

CIRCUS LIQUOR (5600 Vineland Ave., North Hollywood, 818-769-1500) This would normally be an average liquor store selling the usual items, except for the fact that it has the greatest sign in all of the Valley and Los Angeles combined! It's a 35-foot neon clown three times the size of the liquor store. Taking up most of the parking, it really brightens up the otherwise dreary intersection of Burbank Blvd. and Vineland Ave. When I first discovered it in 1987, I made Pleasant (our fearless editor) take a ten-mile ride in my car, blindfolded the whole way from Hollywood, blasting, "Is That All There Is" by Peggy Lee. Just as we arrived in view of the sign, I ripped off the blindfold, and in perfect synchronicity, Peggy Lee was singing, "Is that all there is to a circus?" Now I'm sure if I was a guy, Pleasant would have proposed to me right then and there. The neighborhood is a little dodgy but worth the risk.

IKEA (600 N. San Fernando Blvd., Burbank, 818-842-4532, www.ikea.com) Doesn't Ikea mean "fancy milk crates" in Swedish? Upwardly mobile furniture for miles! Now, here's a place that should have rest stops.

BARNES & NOBLE (Media City Center, 731 N. San Fernando Blvd, 818-558-1383, www.barnesandnoble.com) Great place for coffee and reading books you'll never buy, in large comfy chairs, which by the way, are always taken. I'm convinced that there's a small family living in the chairs in the front window lobby area.

HANDMADE (14556 Ventura Blvd, Sherman Oaks, 818-382-344) If a flea market and a garage sale had a baby you'd get Handmade. The best collection of handmade and imported merchandise, filling a huge-ass warehouse. Where punk rock meets Birkenstock. Dishware, clothing, vintage jewelry, distressed wood furniture, Buddha-shaped dresses, Curious George lunch boxes, Dirty Girl bath products, stationery for "Bad Boys," and featuring the really cool line of Skellramics (www.skellramics.com) for all your skull needs.

RAGTIME COWBOY (5213 Lankershim Blvd., N. Hollywood, 818-769-6552) Joe (the owner) has been dubbed the "Fashion Guru of NoHo," but he's so much more than that! Whatever you need, Joe has it: Great vintage clothing mixed with hats, shoes, antique quilts and bedspreads, glamour wigs, clown wigs, clown suits, Frankenstein shoes, and costumes that you didn't even know existed but that you must have immediately. The prices are amazing and Joe immediately makes you feel like you've known him all your life! We love Joe!

HISTORIC AND CULT POINTS OF INTEREST

Spahn Ranch The location that the **Manson Family** lived and fled to during the Tate-LaBianca murders in 1969. Located along the south side of Santa Susanna Pass Road near the entrance to Iverson Movie Ranch, the movie/tourist sets burned down in the wildfires of 1970. Since that time, the property has been subdivided into at least three separate parcels. I once went there with writer Legs McNeil and skinhead rednecks chased us out. Kind of fitting.

Topanga Canyon The anti-establishment, hippie settling ground. Known for pagan rituals, VW buses with tie-dyed flags, witches, Love-Ins, Indians, members of the Manson Family, UFO and Jim Morrison sightings. In the '20s, Hollywood stars were known to have hideaway cabins for secret affairs, some of which are probably still standing. During War II, mobster Mickey Cohen owned and operated a casino and brothel here. In the '50s, artists and intellectuals lived here waiting out the McCarthy era. In the '70s, Topanga Canyon became the home for the likes of **Neil Young, Gram Parsons, the Eagles**, and **Linda Ronstadt**. It's still a beautiful, curve-filled ride from the Valley to the Ocean.

Lake View Terrace Put on the map as a result of being the site of the famous **Rodney King** beating, which led to the LA Riots in '92.

405 Freeway That historic drive featuring **OJ Simpson** in a white Bronco down the 405 freeway with a gun held to his head pleading his innocence in the Nicole Brown Simpson and Ron Goldman murders. And just so ya know, avoid it at all costs during rush hour (the only time it's NOT rush hour is from 12–1 p.m. daily), it turns into a parking lot! It takes 4 or 5 hours to get anywhere.

Reseda   A nowhere spot on the road, until the January 17, **1994 earthquake** shook it into the headlines... was also used as the back drop for the setting of the film *Boogie Nights*.

Burbank   Home of the Mob and the Mod. In 1952, the California crime commission singled out Burbank as being a hangout for the Mafia. In the 1960s, more popularly known for being tagged "Beautiful Downtown Burbank" on the popular variety show *Laugh In* and also *The Tonight Show* starring Johnny Carson.

Pacoima   Singer **Ritchie Valens** was born and raised in Pacoima. On February 3, 1959, at the age of 17 was killed in a historic plane crash along with rock'n'roll legends Buddy Holly and the Big Bopper.

North Hollywood   Now called the NoHo Arts District, formerly known as "The Porn Capital of the World."

Canoga Park   The Porn Capital of the World.

THE BLACK DAHLIA DRANK HERE
Iris Berry

Being a native Los Angeles girl, I've always been fascinated with old Hollywood and old LA. I'm in love with a city that doesn't exist anymore: I miss the historical monuments and places that should have (but didn't) make it and are now gone forever. Some of my favorite places have been laid to rest, but fortunately many haven't.

Schwab's Drugstore (8024 Sunset Blvd., Hollywood) once stood where the Virgin Megastore is now. Legend has it that Lana Turner was discovered there, but it isn't true, that was just a great publicity story that refuses to die. I spent many of my teenage days here stealing make-up and sipping coffee at the counter with a wild assortment of Vaudevillian has-beens, many of them promising to make me a star, yeah, right! Currently, at the corner of Sunset and Vine, stands a retail outlet called **Schwab's** (1521 Vine St. 323-462-4300), named, of course, for the famous Schwab's drugstore. As a part of Hollywood's comeback, it includes a lunch counter designed to re-create the look of the original Schwab's, but don't bet on getting discovered there!

The Garden of Allah (8150-52 Sunset Blvd., Hollywood) was a 25-bungalow party house to the stars, and the party lasted 32 years (1927-1959), with such residents as Marlene Dietrich, Humphrey Bogart, Lauren Bacall, the Marx Brothers, Greta Garbo, and F. Scott Fitzgerald. It now exists only as a miniature in a glass case, housed in the bank building where the Garden once stood. I'm sure that I lived there in a past life (and I'm still hungover from it).

Formosa Café (7156 Santa Monica Blvd., West Hollywood, 323-850-9050) Open since 1939, and featured prominently in the movie *LA Confidential*. A Hollywood version of a Chinese restaurant/bar, Philip Marlowe-style. Rumor has it that Elvis once tipped one of the waitresses a Cadillac, not bad for a day's pay. My favorite place for good Chinese food and sick, kitschy celebrity memorabilia.

Farmer's Market (300 N. Fairfax Ave., Los Angeles) LA's oldest outdoor market was built in 1934, and is still one of the more popular tourist destinations. Recently remodeled with an all-new outdoor mall connected to the famous landmark, called "The Grove." Complete with movie theatres, fountains with dancing waters, FAO Schwartz, Nordstrom, and so much more... a little new world with your old world. Farmer's Market has Hollywood souvenirs in every shape and form. One of my favorite places to eat, and buy stuff like key chains, salt and pepper shakers, fresh fruit, and toffee.

Bullocks Wilshire (3050 Wilshire Blvd. Miracle Mile/ Mid City) Art Deco masterpiece built in 1929. The first "suburban" department store in the United States. It managed to stay open through the culturally devoid 1980s, complete with valet parking and Chandleresque elevator men. No longer open for business, it still stands looking quite regal. I have fond memories of eating lunch with my mother in their exquisite Tea Room on the top floor, occasionally being interrupted at the table by a fashion model displaying the latest in Chanel, with a view of the city all around.

Magic Castle (7001 Franklin Ave., Hollywood, www.magiccastle.com, 323-851-3313) A private club for magicians and those who appreciate magic. Built in 1909, it resembles a Victorian haunted mansion, and houses a restaurant, three theaters, a museum, and library. They also give magic classes and seminars. My goal is to one day be sawed in half here...

2nd Street Tunnel (located underneath Bunker Hill, Downtown LA) One city block long. Many a famous car chase has been filmed through this tunnel. It was my first tunnel experience as a small child. My goal is to one day be chased through here.

Paramount Studios (5555 Melrose Ave., Hollywood, 323-956-5575) The last big name studio still actually located in Hollywood. One of my first jobs was here... although somehow I managed to never do my work and never get caught. I would lock my office door and climb out of my window to do things like hang out with the cast of "Happy Days," watching them play basketball with Nick Nolte while drinking champagne with the Fonz. That was a great job. My goal is to one day get rehired here.

Hollywood Roosevelt Hotel (7000 Hollywood Blvd., Hollywood, 323-466-7000) Located right on the Walk of Fame, across from Graumann's Chinese Theatre. For the true Hollywood experience, book yourself a room in this twelve-story, Spanish-style hotel built in 1927. The Clark Gable/Carol

Lombard suite is only $1500 a night... yeah right! My goal is to either afford to stay here one day or haunt here, whichever comes first.

Musso & Frank's Grill (6667 Hollywood Blvd., Hollywood, 323-467-5123) Oldest restaurant in Hollywood, since 1919. In the '30s and '40s, it was a famous hangout for writers like William Faulkner, F. Scott Fitzgerald, and Budd Schulberg. To this day, it has the finest reputation for its food and atmosphere. As the saying goes, "After God made the world, he rested at Musso's." Dining here on my 25th birthday, Pleasant had me paged over the intercom. When I picked up the phone, she whispered, "So, do you feel important?" Definitely a good place to get paged.

Angel's Flight (Northwest corner of Third and Hill Streets, Downtown) This is one of the rare examples where LA has rebuilt a landmark it once tore down. The two-car railway goes from Hill Street up to Bunker Hill. The view from the top is my favorite LA view.

Echo Park (1100 block Echo Park Ave. Echo Park) Like most city parks that have their own lake, this one provides a romantic paddleboat ride with a front-row picturesque view of the Downtown Los Angeles skyline. My favorite first date took place here.

Philippe the Original (1001 N. Alameda St., Downtown, 323-628-3781, www.philippes.com) Original home of the French Dip Sandwich, in business since 1908. A cup of coffee is still only ten cents (take that, Starbucks!) My favorite place for a good lamb dip sandwich and old circus photos.

Hollywood Forever Memorial Park (6000 Santa Monica Blvd., Hollywood, 323-469-1181, www.hollywood forever.com) Formerly known as Hollywood Cemetery, this is the final resting place for folks like Bugsy Siegel, Rudolph Valentino, Tyrone Power, Virginia Rappe, Douglas Fairbanks,

Peter Lorre and many other stars, as well as a number of Armenian Mafia dons. One of my least favorite first dates took place here.

Hollywood Bowl (2301 Hollywood Blvd., Hollywood, 323-850-2000, www.hollywoodbowl.com) Famous for its musical events of many different varieties, from rock to jazz and classical to the yearly Mariachi Festival. I saw Donovan here with my mom when I was 10 years old and got my first contact high from all the pot smoke.

Baroque Books (1643 Las Palmas Blvd. Hollywood) Once a great bookstore for all the classics, owned by legend Red Stodolsky. I bought my first Bukowski book here, and at one time it was the only place where you could get his books. The store closed down years ago when Red passed away, leaving a huge hole in the city, but his spirit still lives on.

The Frolic Room (6245 Hollywood Blvd., Hollywood, 323-462-5890, www.bobsfrolicroom.com) You can't miss this place, it's got some of the best neon in town, and has been featured in a number of films. A little closet of a bar right smack dab next to the Pantages Theatre, known for its Hirshfeld wallpaper with caricatures of Jayne Mansfield, Frank Sinatra, the Marx Brothers, and Laurel and Hardy to name a few, whooping it up. If you're looking for old Hollywood, the Frolic Room is one of the last holdouts. This is one of my favorite places to read bathroom graffiti.

Miceli's Restaurant (1646 Las Palmas Blvd. Hollywood, 323-466-3438, www.venturablvd.com/micelis) One of the older Hollywood restaurants still around. Great Italian food and great atmosphere. I love to eat dinner here at twilight with the view of the Las Palmas bookstand through the stained glass windows. It's like stepping back in time.

Bob's Big Boy (4211 Riverside Drive, Toluca Lake, 818-843-9334, www.bobs.net) With its running tradition since

1958, every Friday night is Cruise Night. The parking lot is crawling with custom cars and hot rods. After my high school reunion ended in a brawl that I was responsible for (the police had to come and break it up), we all came here to eat and talk about how much fun we had. Now that's a memory I'll always cherish.

Cinerama Dome Theatre (6360 Sunset Blvd., Hollywood, 323-464-4226) The world's first Cinerama theatre with a unique shape, a huge white dome looking a lot like half a giant golf ball. Recently remodeled and now attached to the Arclight Theatre and a brand new modern mall. Pity... but at least it wasn't torn down, as was the original plan! My mother took my babysitter and me her to see *Easy Rider* when it first came out.

About the Authors

IRIS BERRY is a widely published author, a recording artist whose discography includes both musical and spoken word recordings, and an actress who can be seen starring in numerous independent films. In addition to keeping up her image as a bottle blonde bombshell, she manages to find time to indulge in her passion for Mexican wrestling and can be frequently spotted at LA Dodgers games. www.irisberry.com

JAYSON MARSTON currently lives in Los Angeles with his amazing wonderdog, Buster. He will be leaving the sharks and the chardonnay of Los Angeles for the bears and ale of Portland.

DEADLEE is a rapper, actor, comedian, counselor, Republican Presidential candidate 2012, mama's boy, Pabst Blue Ribbon drinker, pig ear sandwich eater, Catholic School Altar Boy, Bench warmer football player. www.deadlee.com

LIBBY MOLYNEAUX writes for the *LA Weekly*. Her husband, Joe Hill, is an avid bike rider throughout the hills of Laurel Canyon.

S.A. GRIFFIN lives and works in The City of Angels, and much to his devoted wife's regret, he cannot imagine living anywhere else. Widely published poet, working actor 30 years, and co-editor of the *Outlaw Bible of American Poetry*. Father, husband, friend, Vietnam-era vet, Cadillac wrangler, crash vampire, and human being. Awards and taxes.

MARY HERZOG reads and writes for a living, and does it all in Silver Lake, because it's awesome there. No offense to Altadena, of course.

MARGARET CHO is a comedian, author, designer, filmmaker and dancer. In 1999 her groundbreaking one-woman show, *I'm The One That I Want*, was turned into a best-selling book and a concert film. She has been nominated for a Grammy, frequently writes for many publications, is an avid social activist, and has been pursuing a growing passion for Middle Eastern Dance and Burlesque for the past few years. www.margaretcho.com

PLEASANT GEHMAN is the author and/or editor of many books, including *Escape from Houdini Mountain*, also published by Manic D Press. She has written extensively about pop culture, arts and entertainment for *LA Weekly, Los Angeles Magazine, LA City Beat* and numerous other publications. She is also an actress, singer, painter and, as Princess Farhana, a professional bellydancer. Pleasant often entertains the notion of leaving Los Angeles, but has lived happily within view of the Hollywood Sign for the past thirty years. www.princess farhana.com / www.plezonline.com.

ANDREA FERRANTE is a perpetually underemployed writer/photographer and bohemian bon vivant. She resides in

East Hollywood where she enjoys reading, cooking for friends, and sipping bourbon with boys that look like chimney sweeps.

LINA LECARO is an LA (Silver Lake, even!) native who has gone from haunting LA after dark with a fake ID at 16, to documenting it as a not-yet-jaded 30-something in mags and rags such as the *LA Weekly*, the *LA Times*, *Flaunt*, *Paper* and *Urb*. Her misadventures are chronicled regularly in her *LA Weekly* column *Nightranger* and on the fashion and lifestyle blog *The Style Council* at www.laweekly.com

RYAN LEACH writes for *Razorcake* and *Punk Planet*. He is obsessive about collecting records, books, and music by Gene Clark, the Byrds and the Gun Club. His favorite bassist is Rob Ritter (AKA Rob Graves). Currently, Ryan is playing bass in Thee Mad Lovers. He can't fight, is a lousy drinker, and self-effacing is his middle name.

AL RIDENOUR (aka "Reverend Al") has written on culture for the *Los Angeles Times*, *Maxim*, *Stuff*, *FHM*, *Saveur*, and is the author of *Offbeat Food: Adventures in an Omnivorous World* (Santa Monica Press). His current project is The Art of Bleeding, an ambulance-based performance troupe dedicated to providing disturbingly unorthodox theatrical programs in safety education. www.artof bleeding.com

E.A. GEHMAN is a writer who "lives" in Los Angeles. She desperately hopes that YOU don't move here after your tragic little visit. Please go bug the crap out of some other over-subscribed metropolis, huh? Kiss-Kiss!

KAREN CUSOLITO is a native Angeleno who used to prowl the streets as a crime reporter for the late, great Los Angeles *Herald Examiner*. She now teaches English at the world famous Hollywood High School.

PAMELA DES BARRES is a best-selling author, renowned journalist, Internet columnist, rock & roll aficionado, and carries the royal title "Queen of the Groupies." A member of the infamous all-girl band, The GTO's, she has been featured on records and CDs, on television, in films, and at the age of forty, was the subject of a fabulous pictorial in *Playboy* magazine.

Index

Bars

Clubs — DJs & Live Performance

Religion

Restaurants, Bakeries, & Cafés